Welcome to Portland

1

T0163894

WORLD AFFAIRS
COUNCIL
DAVID BROOKS

Arlene Schnitzer Concert Hall
© Ludovic Maisant/hemis.fr

Getting to Portland

BY PLANE

Portland International Airport (PDX) – ✆ (503) 460 4234 – www.flypdx.com. The state's main airport is located east of the I-5, around a 20min drive from the center of Portland. There are restaurants, shops, currency exchanges and car rental counters at the airport. ♿ *Airlines, p. 102.*

Access the city center
Take the TriMet **MAX Light Rail** (daily 5am-midnight, $2.50). Allow 40min. **Uber** and **Lyft** both pick up at PDX. You can also book ahead of time with **Wingz** (www.wingz.me/airport/pdx). There are several shuttle companies (see www.flypdx.com/groundtransportation/shuttle). Some hotels offer free airport shuttles (see website above). **Taxis** cost around $40. ♿ *Taxis, p. 117.*

BY TRAIN

Amtrak – ✆ (215) 856 7924 – www.amtrak.com. Three inter-city train lines provide daily connections from Portland to Seattle (3hr30min), Vancouver (4hr), Oakland (1 day) and Chicago (2 days). **Union Station**, Portland's historic train station is located Downtown (***detachable map C4*** – on the corner of NW 6th Ave. and NW Irving St.).

> ### *Go car-free*
> *Portland is one of the few US cities where you can easily get around without a car because of the excellent **public transportation** (♿ p. 116). However, if you want to explore areas outside the city, it's worth renting a car (♿ p. 107).*

BY BUS

Greyhound – Near the train station – 427 NW 6th Ave. – www.greyhound.com. This company provides frequent, albeit very long, connections to Seattle (4hr), Vancouver (8hr), Boise (9hr30min), San Francisco (17hr30min), Denver (28hr) and Chicago (50hr).

3

Columbia sculpture by Larry Kirkland, Portland International Airport
© ivanastar/iStockphoto.com

Unmissable

Our picks for must-see sights

4

Portland Japanese Garden ★★★
Map A5 – 🐾 p. 30

Pearl District ★★
Map C4–5 – 🐾 p. 27

Portland Art Museum ★★
Map C6 – 🐾 p. 21

Portland Saturday Market ★
Map C5 – 🐾 p. 86

International Rose Test Garden ★★
Map A5 – 🐾 p. 30

Oregon Museum of Science and Industry ★★
Map D6–7 – 🕭 p. 40

Lan Su Chinese Garden ★
Map C5 – 🕭 p. 26

Powell's City of Books ★
Map C5 – 🕭 p. 88

5

Mount Hood ★★
Surrounding Area
Map – 🕭 p. 52

Ecola State Park ★★★ and Cannon Beach ★★
Surrounding Area Map –
🕭 p. 63

Our top picks

♥ **As night falls, cross Burnside Bridge and gaze up at the White Stag.** A shining symbol of Portland, this famous neon sign lights up each evening, bringing the promise of an exciting and vibrant night ahead. It also highlights the strong link Portland has with its stunning natural surroundings. *See p. 25.*

♥ **Take a breather at The Grotto gardens** Little known, enchanting and suspended above the city in an Olympian calm, these gardens, run by the Catholic church but open to all, provide a moment of tranquility with views over the flat, snow-capped summit of Mount St. Helens. *See p. 48.*

♥ **Change your perspective at the Center for Native American Art.** This exceptional collection at the heart of Portland Art Museum defies clichés about Native American tribal traditions. The center showcases the modernity, audacity and imagination of contemporary Native American artists. *See p. 22.*

© Jamie Francis/Travel Portland

Forest Park

💚 **See a local band at a neighborhood bar.** Home to a very creative alternative music scene which has given birth to distinctive artists like Elliott Smith, The Dandy Warhols and Johnny Jewel, Portland remains one of the best places on the West Coast to discover new talent over a pre-dinner drink. *See pp. 77 and 92.*

💚 **Treat yourself to a gourmet happy hour.** A foodie heaven, Portland offers more than food carts to those on a shoestring budget. Every evening from around 5pm to 6:30pm, the top restaurants in the city offer reduced menus with prices that won't break the bank. You can't leave Portland without trying its unique craft beverages, nothing like the caffeinated dishwater and sickly-sweet sodas typically served in American diners. *See pp. 66 and 77.*

💚 **Lose yourself in Forest Park's labyrinth of trails.** This is one of the largest forested parks in the US, popular with hikers who can soak up Oregon's spectacular nature without setting foot outside the city. While you're there, make sure to visit Pittock Mansion, an exquisitely furnished manor house from the early 19th century. *See p. 34.*

💚 **Bag yourself a ticket to a roller derby.** This amateur sport played on roller skates is both surprisingly brutal and great fun to watch. The festive match-day atmosphere of the local women's team—the Rose City Rollers—makes for a great evening out with family or friends. *See p. 121.*

💚 **Discover the beaches of the Pacific Coast.** A 1hr30min drive from Portland, Ecola State Park reveals a magnificent panoramic view over the rocks of Cannon Beach, presided over by the mountains. It almost looks as though the forest and its pines are throwing themselves into the ocean. A paradise for surfers, Cannon Beach is equally suited to a relaxing day of sunbathing. While it can be crowded at the weekend, visit mid-week or out of season and you'll get the sublime feeling of being at the edge of the world and (almost) on your own. *See p. 63.*

💚 **Take a step back in time at the fascinating Evergreen Aviation & Space Museum** on the outskirts of McMinnville. Divided between two hangars, one dedicated to the history of aviation and the other to space exploration, this museum houses hundreds of models, including iconic fighter planes from the Second World War. *See p. 60.*

💚 **Try wines from the Willamette and Tualatin Valleys.** Here the pinot noir variety is king. Exceptional terroirs, a long growing season with a dry summer, chilly fall and wet winter, tempered by the proximity to the ocean, create optimum conditions for its growth. *See pp. 54 and 58.*

Portland in 3 days

DAY 1

▶ Morning

Get inspired by the **White Stag** *(p. 25)*, starting in **Old Town★★ and Chinatown** *(p. 24)*, the historic heart of Portland. The imposing cast-iron buildings from the late 19th century around **Skidmore Fountain★** *(p. 24)*, are a beauty to behold as you stroll. If you start this tour on a Saturday or Sunday, make sure to visit the **Portland Saturday Market★** *(p. 86)*. With its wealth of arts and crafts, you can get your hands on some creative buys while getting a feel for this bohemian and eco-friendly city. Drop by **Hoodoo Antiques** *(p. 86)* to admire the charming remnants of bygone eras before heading for the soothing respite that is exquisite **Lan Su Chinese Garden★** *(p. 26)*.

▶ Afternoon

At the **Portland Art Museum★★** *(p. 21)*, your preconceptions about Native art will be swept away in the **Center for Native American Art★★**. You can also marvel at the collections of Impressionist and modern paintings. Continue your cultural journey in the charming Pearl District, more specifically at **Powell's City of Books★** *(p. 88)*, the largest bookstore in the world.

▶ Evening

For the perfect end to the day, head to the fashionable Northwest district and have dinner at **Paley's Place Bistro and Bar** *(p. 69)*, where you can enjoy the very best of American contemporary cuisine in the elegant setting of a Victorian house.

DAY 2

▶ Morning

Enjoy a breath of fresh air and a feast for the eyes at **Washington Park★★★** *(p. 30)*, the vast urban green space whose grounds include the unmissable **Portland Japanese Garden★★★** and **International Rose Test Garden★★** *(p. 30)*, among others. If you're on the lookout for child-friendly activities, don't miss the **Oregon Zoo★★** or the **Portland Children's Museum** *(p. 32)*. Next, cross the Willamette River to

Shopping in the Mississippi district, Eastside

© Jamie Francis/Travel Portland

8

reach the authentic and bohemian **Eastside**★ *(p. 41)*.

▶ *Afternoon*

After savoring Portland's best sandwiches at **Bunk** *(p. 73)* in the vibrant **Alberta Arts District**, there's time for shopping at the artisan retailers of the **Mississippi/Williams** district *(p. 45)*.

▶ *Evening*

Dine at **Ox** *(p. 74)*, in the Northeast district, an Argentinian restaurant and classic favorite. For a bit of rock 'n' roll, round off the night at an Alberta dive bar like **Alleyway** *(p. 82)* or a Central Eastside microbrewery like **Hair of the Dog** or **Base Camp Brewing Company** *(p. 81)*.

DAY 3

▶ *Morning*

Roam the **Central Eastside** industrial quarter and pick up exotic presents from **Cargo** or gourmet delights from **Smith Teamaker** *(p. 89)* and **Jacobsen Salt Co**. *(p. 90)*. Gamers shouldn't miss **Guardian Games** *(p. 89)*, a huge warehouse filled with board and role-playing games. Tuck in to a

Southeast Wine Collective **9**

© Jamie Francis/Travel Portland

brunch of local charcuterie at **Olympia Provisions** *(p. 69)* or an Italian breakfast at the excellent **Clarklewis** *(p. 70)*.

▶ *Afternoon*

Head towards **Southeast** and visit the quirky **National Hat Museum**★ *(p. 42)*, set in a historic home. Wander through the **Division/Clinton** district to pick up some vintage gems at **Xtabay Vintage** and rare records at **Clinton Street Record & Stereo** *(p. 90)*.

▶ *Evening*

Sip on a pre-dinner glass of Oregonian wine at **Bar Norman** *(p. 81)* or at **Southeast Wine Collective** *(p. 72)*, both run by highly talented women. Wind up your visit to the capital of American underground music with an indie rock concert in the **Hawthorne/ Belmont** district at **Liquor Store** *(p. 81)*.

For 2 or 3 more days

If you want to extend your stay and explore the surrounding area, some unforgettable trails (p. 49) can be found less than 2hr's drive away. You should spend at least one day on the coast, one at the Columbia River Gorge and around Mount Hood, and one visiting the Willamette Valley vineyards. Spend one night in each location so you have two days to see each area.

Discovering Portland

Iconic White Stag neon sign near Burnside Bridge
© artran/iStockphoto.com

Portland today

Portland, Oregon. The image that first springs to mind is pure Far West, but also alternative rock, a cycling paradise, mountains with tall misty forests and the trendiest coffee shops. Portland is a raw industrial city that enjoys an intoxicating, undefinable charm. Could it be its bucolic atmosphere? Its laid-back inhabitants? Its gentle way of life? Its touching weirdness? Taxi drivers will tell you that you only have to visit Portland twice to fall in love. The third time, you'll be here for life.

Bohemian and gentrified

Portland is the new capital of cool on the West Coast, attracting hipsters from around the world. A generation of creative, hip, connected 24/7, eco-conscious young people seems to have invaded the third wave cafés, artisan distilleries and vintage boutiques. An alternative current has been around in Portland for a long time. In the 1960s, low rents attracted penniless artists and others turning their backs on consumer society. In the 90s, an underground music scene—the birthplace of innovative bands like The Dandy Warhols, Pink Martini and, later on, the Chromatics—flourished in countless bars, while independent filmmakers, led by Gus Van Sant, rewrote the rulebook of American cinema. The city's inevitable gentrification started with the arrival of start-ups in the early aughts. From that moment onwards, with Adidas, Nike and Intel's headquarters taking root in the city, Portland has seen its rents skyrocket and its industrial warehouses converted into state-of-the-art offices. Around Washington Park, the discreet villas of millionaires overlook the city.

You can still find a blend of bohemian atmosphere in a few neighborhoods: eastern Portland; the districts of Division/Clinton, Alberta Arts District, Hawthorne/Belmont and Laurelhurst. Old squats and concert halls are still the setting of a vibrant, frenzied cultural scene. The popular slogan 'Keep Portland Weird' is taken at face value by many locals: you may catch sight of someone playing the bagpipes perched on a motorbike or doomsday fanatics spouting their beliefs in the streets, and no one bats an eyelid!

An enclave of tolerance

Open-mindedness is a character trait that all Portlanders have in common. Here, being laid-back is the order of the day, as illustrated by the joke: "What do you call someone wearing a suit in Portland?" Answer: "A tourist!" Portlanders dress casually in jeans and T-shirts. They're always ready to jump on their bikes or set off on a camping trip in the mountains. Above all, they never raise their voices and agree with everything that is said to them, even if they secretly disagree. This agreeable attitude, called 'quietly judging,' lets everyone lead their lives as they see fit. A tolerant city, both in terms of religion (42% of the population is atheist or agnostic)

Photo by NashCO/Travel Portland

Portland State University market

and sexual orientation (it has the second largest LGBTQ community after San Francisco), Portland is also a Democratic enclave in a predominantly Republican-voting Oregon.

A green oasis

These political stances go hand in hand with a deep-rooted environmental awareness. Portland has been actively managing its urban planning since the 1960s. The Urban Growth Boundary, launched by governor Tom McCall in 1973, has steered the city's growth towards developing residential areas rather than industrial ones, limiting highways and preserving agricultural land. A major commercial port and industrial city with significant steel production, Portland remains fully in sync with the nature that surrounds it. The vast mountains and forests found around the city are well-loved by Portlanders who take every opportunity to escape for hikes. The long, gray winters are forgotten with the first rays of spring sunshine, tempting you out on adventures. From Mt. Hood to Mt. Rainier, the soil is fertile and Oregon's agriculture—local and often organic—has given rise to a foodie scene creative and locavore, ready to delight vegetarians, carnivores and vegans alike.

Whether you're a young gourmand or older hipster, a nature lover or indie rock fan, whether you visit by yourself, with friends or family, Portland has a few tricks up its sleeve to captivate you with seeming effortlessness.

Downtown★

Lively and a pleasant size to explore on foot, Portland's city center is made up of two distinct areas. First, in the Pioneer District, you'll find luxury boutiques, department stores, offices, restaurants and hotels concentrated around Pioneer Courthouse Square. Second, the Cultural District spans twelve city blocks around South Park Blocks, a green oasis surrounded by museums and venues for cultural performances, including the Oregon Historical Society and Portland Art Museum. Downtown is also the student heart of the city with Portland State University and a 50-acre campus that welcomes some 30,000 students.

▶ **Access:** The city center is located between the Willamette River to the east and I-405 to the west. If you're traveling by car, park on the east side of the Willamette, which is less expensive than the west. You can easily return on foot, crossing one of the city's numerous bridges (👣 *p. 36).*
Area map pp. 16–17. Detachable map BC5–7.
▶ **Tip:** If you're in a rush, opt for the Portland Art Museum and a food cart lunch.
👣 *Addresses pp. 66, 77, 85 and 95.*

14

PIONEER COURTHOUSE SQUARE★

C5 Fondly referred to as "Portland's living room," this square was built following the destruction of the palatial 20th-century Portland Hotel, and narrowly escaped being turned into a parking lot. The square is surrounded by skyscrapers, some built around 1910, including the picturesque **Jackson Tower** with its monumental clock tower and the elegant **Meier & Frank Building** with its terracotta-clad facades, and some from the 80s.
The **Pioneer Courthouse**★ is a fine stone building built in 1869 in a Neoclassical style. It has been a courthouse since 1875. Do venture inside (Mon-Fri 9am-4pm) to admire the view from the cupola, over the square and the surrounding buildings.

BROADWAY★

C5–6 Flanked by historical skyscrapers, hotels and restaurants, and crossing Downtown from north to south, this main thoroughfare slopes gently up to Portland State University. The most emblematic buildings include **The Benson** (👣 *p. 95),* built in 1913 in an eclectic French-Italian style by Simon Benson, one of the city's first patrons. Open the doors to this prestigious hotel and catch a glimpse of its splendid lobby. Then, further up the street, discover the **Arlene Schnitzer Concert Hall** (👣 *p. 92),* a vast Art Deco theater, built in 1928 and recognizable for its sign, emblematic

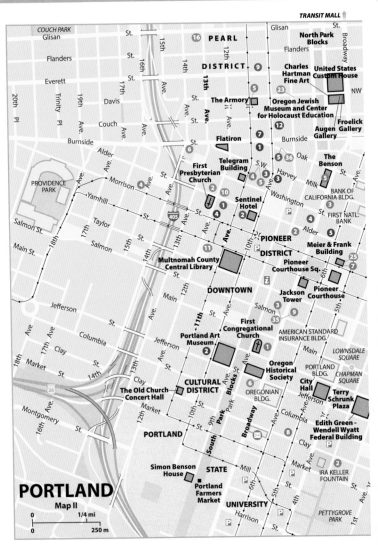

TRANSIT MALL

COUCH PARK
Glisan St.

Glisan St.

PEARL

Flanders St.

North Park Blocks

Everett

Davis

Couch

Burnside St.

DISTRICT

Charles Hartman Fine Art

United States Custom House

NW

The Armory

Oregon Jewish Museum and Center for Holocaust Education

Froelick Gallery

Augen Gallery

Flatiron

Burnside

First Presbyterian Church

Telegram Building

Oak

The Benson

PROVIDENCE PARK

Alder Ave.

Morrison

Harvey

BANK OF CALIFORNIA BLDG.

Yamhill St.

Sentinel Hotel

Washington

Milk

FIRST NATL. BANK

Taylor

Salmon

PIONEER

Meier & Frank Building

Main St.

Salmon St.

DOWNTOWN

Multnomah County Central Library

DISTRICT

Pioneer Courthouse Sq.

Pioneer Courthouse

16

Jefferson

Main

Jackson Tower

Salmon

Columbia

First Congregational Church

AMERICAN STANDARD INSURANCE BLDG.

LOWNSDALE SQUARE

Clay

Portland Art Museum

Market

CULTURAL DISTRICT

Oregon Historical Society

OREGONIAN BLDG.

PORTLAND BLDG.

CHAPMAN SQUARE

City Hall

Terry Schrunk Plaza

The Old Church Concert Hall

Clay

Edith Green – Wendell Wyatt Federal Building

Montgomery St.

PORTLAND

Market

Jefferson

Columbia

Clay

PORTLAND

Map II

Simon Benson House

STATE

Mill

IRA KELLER FOUNTAIN

Portland Farmers Market

UNIVERSITY

Harrison St.

PETTYGROVE PARK

0   1/4 mi

0   250 m

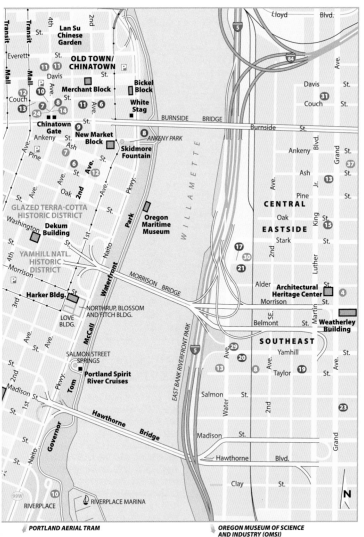

PORTLAND AERIAL TRAM

OREGON MUSEUM OF SCIENCE AND INDUSTRY (OMSI)

of Portland. It's the last surviving theater on Broadway.

SOUTH PARK BLOCKS ★

BC6 This tree-lined avenue with its lawns, statues of famous figures and water points is Downtown's precious green oasis. It's surrounded by important Portland institutions including major museums and the **First Congregational Church** (1899), whose elegant bell tower is built in Venetian Gothic style.

OREGON HISTORICAL SOCIETY ★★

C6 *1200 SW Park Ave. – ☏ (503) 222 1741 – www.ohs.org – ♿ – Mon-Sat 10am–5pm, Sun noon–5pm – $10 (under 18s: $5).*
Looking back on Lewis and Clark's expedition and the historic **Oregon Trail** (♿ p. 126), an eight-story-tall *trompe-l'œil* mural marks the entrance to this museum, dedicated to Oregon's history. The **Oregon Voices★** exhibition lets you discover accounts from

> ## *Benson Bubblers, iconic drinking fountains*
> *Downtown, and particularly around Pioneer Courthouse, you'll notice entertaining drinking fountains with four jets of water falling into bronze bowls. Dreamed up in 1912 by Simon Benson, a rich businessman and Portland benefactor, these allow you to quench your thirst for free alongside others, without having to wait your turn. Now one of the city's symbols, the Benson Bubblers serve fresh, pure, non-recycled water. Since 1992, the city has drastically reduced their flow to make them more eco-friendly.*

Oregon's inhabitants from the 1950s to the present day through interactive presentations. The building's lower floor houses temporary exhibitions.

THE OLD CHURCH CONCERT HALL

B6 *1422 SW 11th Ave. – www.theold church.org – Free concert Wed noon.* The city's oldest church (1882), in Neo-Gothic style, impresses with its elegant white wooden facades and delicate bell tower topped with a spire. It has been converted into a concert hall.

PORTLAND STATE UNIVERSITY

BC6 Don't miss out on a Saturday morning stroll here through the colorful **Portland Farmers Market** (♿ *p. 86*). The campus itself is very pleasant and can easily be explored on foot. At the entrance, at the top of South Park Blocks, look out for the **Simon Benson House**★ *(1803 SW Park Ave.)*, a Queen Anne-style building that dates back to 1900. This house was built a few blocks from its present location, but like many old Portland houses, it was moved here in 2000 to be restored. Built out of light-colored wood with a pergola and subtle decorations, it invites you inside to discover its beautiful, well-preserved

historic features, like the dining room and the staircase. It houses the university's alumni association and is only open on weekdays.

TERRY SCHRUNK PLAZA

C6 Two very different buildings face each other over this vast tree-filled esplanade. On one side is **City Hall**

© P. Orain/Michelin

Simon Benson House

(1895) with its classic rotunda; on the other is the **Edith Green – Wendell Wyatt Federal Building**★ (1220 SW 3rd Ave.). This skyscraper (361 ft tall,) was completely remodeled between 2009 and 2013. The facade is now clad in a glass and metal mesh, optimizing its exposure to sunlight. Its high energy performance led the building to be named one of the top 10 US sustainable projects of 2015.

AROUND SOUTHWEST 11TH AVENUE AND ALDER STREET

C5–6 In this pleasant commercial district, you can admire some of Portland's iconic buildings. The **Central Library** (801 SW 10th Ave.) is the largest library in Oregon and was built in 1913 in the Georgian style. The **Sentinel Hotel** (🔊 p. 96)— previously known as the Elks Temple after the fraternal order that built it in 1923—is imposing with its four-story **monumental facade**★ in the style of an Italian Renaissance palace. On the corner of Alder Street and SW 12th Ave., you will notice the **First Presbyterian**

Church (1886) with its Victorian-Gothic bell tower topped with a high spire. On the corner of SW Washington Street and SW 11th Ave. is the outstanding **Telegram Building** (1922), whose white American colonial-style bell tower will stand out spectacularly against the blue sky in photos. On the wall across the street (a housing block now converted into a parking garage) you will see a beautiful and intriguing **mural** depicting a woman with her back to you; Capax Infiniti is a work by the South African artist **Faith47**. You can finish your walk between **Union Way**, a contemporary-style shopping arcade (🔊 p. 85), and the **Flatiron**: this little gem, located on the corner of Harvey Milk St. and West Burnside St., is home to the café Ringlers Annex.

PORTLAND ART MUSEUM★★

C6 1219 SW Park Ave. – ✆ (503) 226 2811 – portlandartmuseum.org – ✕ ♿ 🅿 – Tue-Sun 10am–5pm (8pm Thur–Fri) - $20 (under 18s: free). The oldest (1892) art gallery on the West Coast is housed in a low brick

20

10 unmissable works of art at the Portland Art Museum

- *Madame de Nittis* (1872) — Edgar Degas
- *The Seine at Argenteuil* (1874) — Pierre-Auguste Renoir
- *Garden View, Rouen* (1884) — Paul Gauguin
- *Hélène is Restless* (1890) — Mary Cassatt
- *The Black Hat* (1900) — Julian Alden Weir
- *The Widow* (1913) — Gertrude Käsebier
- *Brook* (1961) — Lois Dodd
- *Stretcher Frame* (1968) — Roy Lichtenstein
- *Blue Savanna* (1978) — Dahlov Ipcar
- *Stampede* (1989) — Annette Lemieux

The musicians who call Portland home

Portland is the birthplace of loads of American indie rock and pop singers and bands. Here are a few musicians who live there. For more on music in Portland, see Nightlife ⚜ p. 29

- *Modest Mouse (formed 1992)*
- *Pink Martini (1994)*
- *The Dandy Warhols (1994)*
- *The Shins (1996)*
- *Laura Veirs (1999)*
- *The Decemberists (1999)*
- *Portugal. The Man (2004)*
- *She & Him (2006)*

building with travertine trim (1992, Pietro Belluschi). With over 18,000 pieces, the exhibitions and installations rotate. Take your time to walk through the numerous rooms and in a couple of hours you'll have an overview of different currents in art from the sculptures and porcelain of East Asia (China, Korea, Japan, 14–19th c.) to **contemporary art★**, such as works by Damien Hirst (*5 Skulls*, 2010). You'll also have the pleasure of admiring delicate Kütahya ceramics (Turkey, 16–20th c.). Beyond works by famous French Impressionists in the **European art section★** and a selection of the masters of modern painting, discover the history of the US through drawings and paintings from the 19th and 20th centuries. Admire the beautiful landscapes of Oregon by Neo-impressionist artist Childe Hassam as well as landscapes by Albert Bierstadt and Thomas Moran.

The museum features two unique centers: the **Center for Northwest Art**, which showcases local artists, and the enthralling **Center for Native American Art★★**, which displays works by over 200 Native American cultural groups, from prehistory to contemporary art, with a selection of extremely original art that can at times be surprising. Outside, a sculpture hall displays works by Henry Moore, Barbara Hepworth and Pierre-Auguste Renoir. An expansion project has been announced that will join the two buildings. Dedicated to Mark Rothko, whose family emigrated to Portland from Russia when he was 10, it will house works by the artist and a reception area.

DEKUM BUILDING★

C5 519 SW 3rd Ave. Built in 1892 in Romanesque Revival style, it is one of the city's most impressive old skyscrapers. The higher brick stories with their series of arcades contrast with the roughly hewed gray stone of the lower stories and monumental doorway.

Old Town★★ *and Chinatown*

The historic heart of Portland, the Old Town district is also home to the city's tiny Chinatown. The entrance is marked by Chinatown Gate, a large archway with five sections built in 1986. Portland's Chinatown is certainly smaller and less active compared to the more established Chinese communities in San Francisco or New York. Old Town still has one of the largest collections of cast-iron buildings in the country, second only to Manhattan's Soho. It's a very lively area, particularly when the Saturday market is on, and its streets makes a lovely walk for 19th-century architecture enthusiasts. Old Town is also home to some of Portland's top restaurants.

▶ **Access:** Old Town is bordered by SW Naito Pkwy, SW Oak St., 3rd Ave. and NW Davis St.; Chinatown by NW 2nd Ave. and 5th Ave., W. Burnside St. and NW Glisan St. **Area map pp. 16–17. Detachable map C4–5.**

▶ **Tip:** Go for a stroll! Check out 19th-century industrial architecture as you walk from the **Portland Saturday Market**★ (🕭 *p. 86*) to Lan Su Chinese Garden, with a doughnut from Voodoo Doughnut for sustenance.
🕭 *Addresses pp. 68, 78, 86 and 96.*

SKIDMORE FOUNTAIN★

C5 Located on the pedestrianized Ankeny Square, this fountain by sculptor **Olin Levi Warner** (1888) is Portland's oldest piece of public art. It was built in memory of Stephen G. Skidmore, a highly regarded pharmacist and benefactor of the city, and styled after fountains Skidmore saw at the Palace of Versailles. The resemblance is not exactly striking, as the fountain is very typical of late 19th-century American architecture, with its clean, Neoclassical lines. A meeting point for Portlanders for a number of events, particularly protests, it is also an excellent landmark to begin a tour of the magnificent cast-iron buildings from the late 19th century that line the streets of Old Town. Take particular note of **Bickel Block** *(33 NW Couch St.)*, dating from 1883. A 2006 renovation revealed the striking cast-iron facades that had been hidden by brick walls. Between the 1850s and 1880s, cast-iron architecture was found on a large scale in most of the big industrial cities. The various components of the buildings —columns, arches, ornaments—were produced in factories, then assembled on site. Cast iron eventually gave way to tougher steel in the late 1880s.

© Iris van den Broek/Shutterstock

Merchant Block

24

SOUTHWEST 2ND AVENUE★

C5 Between Pine Street and Skidmore Fountain, this avenue is lined with old brick, stone and cast iron buildings. Their fine facades, decorated with thousands of details, can be seen on the sober yet elegant **Pine Street Market** (♿ *p. 68*), or the more extravagant Renaissance-style **New Market Block**.

WHITE STAG

C5 *70 NW Couch St.* On the corner of West Burnside and Naito Parkway, check out the enormous "Portland Oregon" sign, which is particularly photogenic at night from Burnside

Bridge. The famous light-up sign has not always been a white stag. Installed in 1940 to advertise White Satin Sugar, it then became an ad for the outerwear brand whose deer seems almost to leap out into the sky. Today, it bears the colors of Portland with pride and, since 1977, has been a symbol of the city. For the Christmas season, a red neon nose is added to the stag in imitation of Rudolph the Red-Nosed Reindeer.

MERCHANT BLOCK★

C5 *131 NW 2nd Ave.* A former chic hotel built in 1880, it is notable for its delicate decoration of cast iron columns, cherubs' heads, its

Shanghai Tunnels

In the late 1850s, kidnappings of drunks doing the rounds of Portland's shady bars were commonplace. The unlucky targets were "shanghaied," or press-ganged, by the captains of boats leaving for Asia. This cynical recruitment practice has given rise to many legends, which are the bread and butter of tourist traps. It is said that the city's underground network of tunnels was used to trap the unlucky "shanghaied," that in the tunnels forced prostitution was rife and there were many illegal opium bars. The lack of scientific evidence has led many historians to believe that the tunnels were simply used to transport goods from the port to warehouses, avoiding the heavy urban traffic of the time.

*Far more captivating than the reality, this legend is the subject of a guided tour, **Underground Portland**, offered by Portland Walking Tours (☎ (503) 774 4522 – www.portlandwalkingtours.com – Meet in front of 131 NW 2ⁿᵈ Ave. – Summer: departs 11am, 2pm and 5pm; rest of the year: departs 10am, weekends 10am and 2pm – $23). Don't expect much more than a damp underground tunnel decorated with objects that could have been bought from a flea market. However, the tour certainly puts the myth into context and provides information about the city's underworld in the late 19th century.*

yellow-beige colors and its outdoor staircases rising up among the trees.

LAN SU CHINESE GARDEN ★

C5 239 NW Everett St. – ☎ (503) 228 8131 – www.lansugarden.org – *From mid-Mar to mid-May: 10am–6pm; from mid-Oct to mid-Mar: 10am–4pm – $10.95 (under 19s: $7.95); from mid-May to mid-Oct: 10am–7pm; $12.95 (under 19s: $9.95).*

This lovely Chinese garden was designed to revive Chinatown and opened in 2002. With its ornamental lakes, bridge-connected pavilions, meditation rooms, and paths that wend their way through the fountains, the Lan Su Chinese Garden, hidden behind high boundary walls, is an oasis of tranquil beauty at the heart of the city. The size of a block of apartments (40,000 ft^2), it has a few real gems; these include a 7,000 ft^2 lake, Taihu, stone rocks (500 tons were imported from China!) and hundreds of Chinese plant species. Make sure you pick up a fact sheet at the entrance to learn about the garden's complex wealth of architecture.

Visitors will find serenity in the garden's excellent **tea room**, housed in the Tower of Cosmic Reflections.

Pearl District★★

Located northwest of Downtown, this trendy district perfectly symbolizes one of the city's pillars: restoring industrial buildings to create functional spaces. Today, this district is a whirlwind of quirky boutiques, art galleries, wine bars and chic restaurants, mostly housed in historical brick buildings. Between shopping sprees, get some fresh air in the district's tranquil green spaces: Tanner Springs Park, with its pond spanned by a small wooden bridge, and Jamison Square, where the cascades of water spill over steps to fill a pool before retreating like the tide.

▶ **Access:** This neighborhood is bordered by W Burnside St., NW 8th Ave. and NW 15th Ave. The Portland tram crosses the heart of Pearl District (10th and 11th Ave.). **Area map pp. 16–17. Detachable map C4–5.**
▶ **Tip:** On the first Thursday of each month, crowds flock to the **First Thursday Gallery Walk** (www.firstthursdayportland.com), which showcases the galleries of this artistic, hip district.
🖈 *Addresses pp. 68, 78 and 88.*

NORTH PARK BLOCKS

C5 NW Park Ave. from Ankeny St. to Glisan St. – 5am–9pm.
The North Park Blocks are identical to the green South Parks Blocks (🖈 *p. 18*) and are found at the heart of the art galleries district. The promenade is also surrounded by major cultural institutions such as the **Pacific Northwest College of Art**, housed in the Neoclassical **Federal Building** (1916). The old, monumental **United States Custom House** has been converted into an extensive coworking space, WeWork.

THE ART GALLERIES★

C5 Some 20 years ago, Pearl District was better known for its rail yards and warehouses battered by the wind

© Travel Portland

Powell's City of Books

A passion for reading

*With **Powell's City of Books★**, the world's largest independent bookstore (☉ p. 88), Portland Book Festival, which attracts thousands of fans each year in November, and the 2016 election of a former bookstore owner to the city council, one thing is sure: Portland certainly loves to read. Here, authors are treated like film stars. Every year, children go head to head in the Oregon Battle of the Books instead of competing in soccer or other popular sports. Are Portlanders bookworms? If you ask them, they'll answer that the climate plays a major role: with eight months of rain a year, it's no wonder they like curling up with a good book!*

and rain. Today, the district is notable for its many art galleries where you might chance upon a Miró, Warhol or Lichtenstein.

Look out for, among others, the **Froelick Gallery** *(714 NW Davis St. – froelickgallery.com – Tue-Sat 10:30am-5:30pm)* which showcases artists with links to Oregon and exhibits works by Native American artists. **Augen Gallery** *(716 NW Davis St. – www.augengallery.com – Tue-Sat 11am-5:30pm)* displays contemporary art. As for **Charles Hartman Fine Art** *(134 NW 8ᵗʰ Ave. – www.hartmanfineart.net – Wed-Sat 11am-5pm)*, its photography collection is superb.

OREGON JEWISH MUSEUM AND CENTER FOR HOLOCAUST EDUCATION★★

C5 *724 NW Davis St. – ✆ (503) 226 3600 – www.ojmche.org – Tue-Fri 11am-5pm (4pm Fri), Sat-Sun noon-5pm – $8 (under 13s: free), free 1ˢᵗ Thur of the month 5pm-8pm.*

There are three permanent exhibitions dedicated to the Jewish diaspora in Oregon in this museum, which opened its doors in 2017. At the heart of the museum is the story of Jewish discrimination and resistance in the state, the Holocaust as told by Oregonian survivors, and an installation on the daily lives of Jews in Oregon. Temporary exhibitions about religious rites, sacred objects and contemporary Jewish art complete a visit to this reasonably sized museum.

THE ARMORY

C5 *128 NW 11ᵗʰ Ave.* Smaller than its older New York cousin, the former Oregon National Guard armory was built in 1891. Its austere facade, which calls to mind a medieval castle, now house two very popular theaters. **Portland Center Stage**, founded in 1998, puts on a range of productions that include both classic and contemporary pieces *(☉ p. 92)*.

NORTHWEST 13ᵀᴴ AVENUE★

C4-5 This street best evokes the district's past, with its immense brick warehouses, raised platforms for unloading goods, and the old painted advertisements that can still be seen on a number of walls. Today, stores, bars and restaurants make it one of the liveliest streets in the Pearl District.

Washington Park★★★

Joining the elegant Arlington Heights neighborhood to the north, this urban oasis snakes its way south over the hillsides bordering western Portland. In its landscaped setting, you'll find several gardens, including the unmissable Japanese garden, as well as an extensive zoo and museums. It's the ideal place for a family outing or to revive yourself with a glorious nature fix, right in the heart of the city. Bordered on the city side by sumptuous houses, it is one of the most fashionable residential neighborhoods in Portland.

▶ **Access:** Enter from the south side of West Burnside Rd and the west of SW Vista Ave. If you want to catch the tram, the Blue and Red lines serve Washington Park MAX station. Bus line 63 takes you to all of the park's attractions. A small shuttle takes zoo visitors to the International Rose Test Garden.
Area map p. 37. Detachable map A5–7 B5–6.

▶ **Tip:** The picnic and play areas dotted around the park are ideal for families with young children. Picnicking is welcome, but know that alcohol is not allowed in the park apart from in the restaurants.

INTERNATIONAL ROSE TEST GARDEN★★

A5 400 SW Kingston Ave. – ☏ (503) 823 3636 – www.portlandoregon.gov/parks – 🅿 – 7:30am–9pm; free guided tour in summer at 1pm (meet in front of the Rose Garden store).

It shouldn't come as a surprise that the city known as the City of Roses has this magnificent experimental rose garden, established in 1917 on the staggered terraces that today overlook the city center. Indulge in the colors and perfumes of 10,000 roses from 600 different varieties. The oldest specimen is from 1943 (Grand Duchess Armstrong, Bed E-23).

PORTLAND JAPANESE GARDEN★★★

A5 611 SW Kingston Ave. – ☏ (503) 223 1321 – www.japanesegarden.com – From mid-Mar to Sept: Mon noon–7pm, Tue–Sun 10am–7pm; from Oct to mid-Mar: Mon noon–4pm, Tue–Sun 10am–4pm – $18.95 (under 18s: $13.50).

If you carry on up the hill, you'll find five meticulously kept acres of Japanese garden whose plants are interspersed with rocks and stretches of water. The landscapes are spellbinding, beautiful and serene, perfect for meditation. It is renowned for being the most authentic Japanese garden outside of Japan. Don't miss

the picturesque moon bridge, the pavilion gallery and Zen-inspired sand and stone garden. Today, you can also see a series of temple-like buildings with very clean lines, designed by the architect Kengo Kuma. The pleasant **Umami Café**, in its elegant setting of glass and greenery, serves Japanese snacks and cakes accompanied by tea *(10am–7pm – $10/15)*.

HOYT ARBORETUM

A6 4000 SW Fairview Blvd – ℘ (503) 865 8733 – www.hoytarboretum.org – Visitor center: Mon–Fri 9am–4pm, weekend 10am–4pm; park: 5am–10pm – Free.
The arboretum's 190 acres showcase over 2,300 tree species from around the world. Twelve miles of tracks meander through fine specimens of magnolia, oak and maple.

WORLD FORESTRY CENTER DISCOVERY MUSEUM★

A6 4033 SW Canyon Rd – ℘ (503) 228 1367 – www.worldforestry.org – 🅿 – 10am–5pm – Closed Tue and Wed in winter – $7 (under 19s: $5).
This museum is all about sustainable development. Across 20,000 ft^2, interactive collections highlight the important role forests play in the world, particularly those of the Pacific Northwest. Keep an eye out for the entertaining video that will take you on a voyage of discovery in a Russian train, Chinese boat and South African jeep to see forests around the world.

OREGON ZOO★★

A6 4001 SW Canyon Rd – ℘ (503) 226 1561 – www.oregonzoo.org – From late May to early Sept: 9:30am–6pm; rest of the year: 9:30am–4pm – $17.95 (under 12s: $12.95); single entry $5 on 2nd Tue from Sept to May.
With its pleasant, green, shady setting, the Portland Zoo is home to over 230 species, including one of the largest herds of **Asian elephants★** reproducing in captivity. The area dedicated to the California condor (Condors of the Columbia), the largest bird in North America, is one of the few places you can still see this endangered species. The zoo is constantly evolving and new polar bear, rhino and monkey areas are set to open sometime this year and 2021.

PORTLAND CHILDREN'S MUSEUM

A6 4015 SW Canyon Rd – ℘ (503) 223 6500 – www.portlandcm.org – ✕ ♿ 🅿 – 9am–5pm – $11.
Much more than a museum, this is an interactive game space that gives kids the chance to participate, letting them discover the power of water, the world of pottery, theater, chemistry, and many other topics. The museum includes an animal hospital, a huge workshop and an enormous outdoor playground dotted with tree houses, water games and a maze. There's definitely something for everyone here, even if the kids are bursting with energy!

Northwest District★

This neighborhood shares many similarities with the Northwest District in San Francisco. Its narrow, shaded streets are full of stately Victorian buildings, many now converted into boutiques. More suited to foodies than party animals, the neighborhood is home to some of the city's finest restaurants. Northwest 23rd Street is the main shopping street, though Northwest 21st Street, with its numerous bars and charming shops, is a close second. Farther out, Forest Park provides an escape into nature.

▶ **Access:** Around NW 23rd Ave. Easily accessed by the NS tram line from the city center.
Area map p. 37. Detachable map AB3–5.
▶ **Tip:** Want to catch a movie? **Cinema 21**, the city's first independent cinema, can be found at 616 NW 21st Ave. (www.cinema21.com).
♿ *Addresses pp. 69, 80, 88 and 97.*

NOB HILL★

B4 Along the tree-lined arteries that run perpendicular to the 21st and 23rd streets of Nob Hill, a neighborhood also called **Alphabet District**, you'll find the prettiest houses in the area. Homes both tiny and huge, with flowered courtyards, in English or hacienda styles; the diversity and wealth of housing here makes this one of the most charming districts in the city. With its manorial airs, the former Mackenzie House, now **William Temple House** *(615 NW 20th Ave.)*, built completely from stone in 1892, displays the same Romanesque Revival style as the first stories of the Dekum Building *(♿ p. 22)*. **Irving Street** is one of the most spectacular streets in the district, featuring a series of houses—between

© Jaynes Gallery/DanitaDelimont.com/age fotostock
Nob Hill's colorful houses

33

NW 17th and 18th St.—that were built in the English Queen Anne style in 1893. On **NW Overton Street**, between NW 23rd and NW 24th Streets, you can see quaint colorful houses next to an elegant colonial home with rounded front steps across the street from a 1950s-style apartment block. Portland is a city of contrasts, even down to its architecture!

PITTOCK MANSION ★

A5 *3229 NW Pittock Dr. (18min walk from the line 20 bus stop on NW Barnes Rd)* – ℘ *(503) 823 3623 – www. pittockmansion.org –* 🅿 *– Jun-Aug: 10am–5pm; Feb–May and Sept–Dec: 10am–4pm – Guided tour on request – Closed Jan – $12 (under 18s: $8).*

The most sumptuous house in Portland is perched 940 ft up in Southwest Hills, offering a **panoramic view★★** to the east over the city, river and Mount Hood.

This sandstone manor house was built in 1914 in Neo-Renaissance 'French Château' style for Henry Pittock, the owner of *The Oregonian* newspaper. If you're not on a tour *(pick up a map at the entrance)*, you'll have access to 23 of the manor's 44 rooms, allowing you to admire its marble and wood finishings, the luxurious turn-of-the-century furnishings and the then-modern amenities (central heating, elevator, etc.).

The woodland behind the building now forms part of Forest Park. Walkers can also access Washington Park (◐ *p. 30*) by taking the bridge over West Burnside Rd.

FOREST PARK ★

A3–5 ℘ *(503) 223 5449 – www. forestparkconservancy.org – 5am–10pm*

This park, 5,172 acres in size with over 80 miles of criss-crossing pathways, is located in the Tualatin Mountains, to the west of the city center. It lives up to its name: visitors really can expect to be greeted by a wild, lush forest—the largest urban forested park in the US.

It was once inhabited by Native American tribes but was emptied of its population when European settlers arrived in the 19th century. In 1903, the Olmsted brothers, sons of the landscape architect of Central Park in New York, proposed turning the forest into a forest park, but this excellent idea didn't become reality until 1948. Today, it's a lovely place to go for a walk, ride a bike or even go for a horse ride, without leaving the city limits.

THE FREAKYBUTTRUE PECULIARIUM AND MUSEUM

B4 *2234 NW Thurman St.* – ℘ *(503) 227 3164 – www.peculiarium.com – Fri–Mon 11am–6pm – $5.*

If you're looking for the weird side of Portland, this place is for you. This little shop of horrors displays monsters and aliens splattered in fake blood in a humorous, fantasy-like blast from the 1980s rubber past. Great for fans of horror B-movies and kids who love a practical joke.

Along the Willamette River★

The vast, majestic Willamette River flows through the beating heart of Portland. Its twelve bridges have given the city the nickname 'Bridge City'. Both green and industrial, the districts that line the river were nearly converted into the Mount Hood Freeway, but in the 1970s, protests by Portlanders forced the Federal Government to promote a public transport plan instead. Most people visit this area, which isn't very residential, for its attractions, like the Oregon Museum of Science and Industry (OMSI), the pleasant park on the banks of the river and the aerial tram.

▶ **Access:** To make the most of the wide open spaces of this district, rent a bike (& *p. 118*), cycle along the river banks, and feel the wind in your hair!

36 *Area maps* **pp. 16–17 and** *opposite*. **Detachable map CD3–8.**

▶ **Tip:** To get a view of the city from the river, hop on one of **Portland Spirit's boats** (& *p. 120*). They organize boat trips from Salmon Street Springs.

THE BRIDGES★

CD3–8 With their spiderweb-like structure, Portland's bridges add a touch of drama to the city. Their beauty can be admired both by day and by night and they're extremely photogenic. Taking them in on foot, by bike or from a car is an unforgettable Portland experience. Of the eight bridges that span the Willamette, the **Steel Bridge★** (1912), linking Old Town to the Northeast, is the only one that's a through truss, double-deck vertical-lift bridge.

The dark green **Hawthorne Bridge★** (1910) is the oldest vertical lift bridge in the world still in operation. It links the Downtown and Southeast districts.

Tilikum Crossing★ opened in September 2015 and is known as "The Bridge of the People" (*Tilikum* meaning 'people' in Chinook Jargon, a now-extinct Native American language of this area). This elegant cable-stayed bridge is a prime example of Portland's values: it is built from non-polluting materials and is reserved for pedestrians, cyclists and public transport. In the evening it lights up with 178 lights that change color and frequency depending on the speed, depth and temperature of the river. It links the Portland State University campus to the Eastside.

St. Johns Bridge★ in the north of the city is also worth a visit (& *p. 46*).

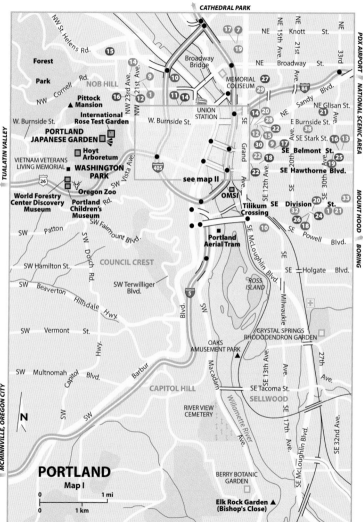

CATHEDRAL PARK

NW St. Helens Rd.

17 7

NE 15th Ave

NE Knott St.

NE 21st

NE 33rd

POX AIRPORT

COLUMBIA RIVER GORGE NATIONAL SCENIC AREA

15

Broadway Bridge

19

NE Broadway St.

NW Cornell Rd.

NOB HILL

14

9

10

MEMORIAL COLISEUM

27

NE Sandy Blvd.

I-84

Forest

Park

Pittock ▲ Mansion

16

NW 23rd Ave.

NW 121st Ave.

12

11 14

29

UNION STATION

14 20

NE Glisan St.

21

International Rose Test Garden

W. Burnside St.

W. Burnside St.

SE

28

E Burnside St.

PORTLAND JAPANESE GARDEN

12 15

SE Stark St.

16 13

Grand

30 9

SE 20th

25

Hoyt Arboretum

Vista Ave.

405

22

18

SE Belmont St.

Vietnam Veterans Living Memorial

WASHINGTON PARK

22

SE 12th

19

SE Hawthorne Blvd.

26

see map II

33

World Forestry Center Discovery Museum

Oregon Zoo

OMSI

SE Division St.

20

32

24

21

1

MOUNT HOOD

BORING

Portland Children's Museum

Tilikum Crossing

26

18

10

SE Powell Blvd.

37

SW Fairmount Blvd.

SW Patton

SW Dosch Rd.

COUNCIL CREST

Portland Aerial Tram

SE McLoughlin Blvd.

SE Holgate Blvd.

SW Hamilton St.

ROSS ISLAND

SW Beaverton Hillsdale Hwy.

SW Terwilliger Blvd.

5

Blvd.

SW

Milwaukie Ave.

CRYSTAL SPRINGS RHODODENDRON GARDEN

27th Ave.

SW Vermont St.

OAKS AMUSEMENT PARK

Macadam

SE 13th Ave.

SW Multnomah Blvd.

SW Capitol Blvd.

Barbur

CAPITOL HILL

SE Tacoma St.

SELLWOOD

SE 17th Ave.

SE 32nd Ave.

N

RIVER VIEW CEMETERY

Willamette River Ave.

SE McLoughlin Blvd.

26

PORTLAND

Map I

BERRY BOTANIC GARDEN

Elk Rock Garden ▲ (Bishop's Close)

0 _____ 1 mi

0 _____ 1 km

GOVERNOR TOM MCCALL WATERFRONT PARK★

C5–7 Between Marquam Bridge and Steel Bridge. This 37-acre grassy park sprawls along the two-mile promenade on the banks of the Willamette. Once upon a time, it was the location of Portland's noisy river port. In the 1970s, as part of an urban renewal plan, the city reclaimed the land. It was named after **Tom McCall** (1913–1983), the state's governor from 1967 to 1975 and the original promoter of the plan. A well-loved playground for joggers and cyclists, this park also holds concerts and festivals like the **Rose Festival** (🕭 *p. 121*).

OREGON MARITIME MUSEUM

C5 SW Naito Parkway, level with Pine St. – ✆ (503) 224 7724 – *oregonmaritimemuseum.org – Wed–Sat 11am–4pm – $7 (under 13s: $3).* Moored at Waterfront Park, the *Portland*, a boat from 1947, is the oldest steam-powered sternwheel tugboat built in the US. It towed merchant ships in the port until the 1980s, when it was converted into a museum. The guided tour *(45min)* gives you an idea of the importance of maritime life in Portland. You can visit the captain's cabin and engine room and see scale models of boats.

YAMHILL DISTRICT★

C6 All along **Southwest 1st Avenue**, there are still fine examples of late-19th-century houses. Surrounded by colorful facades, an inscription on the charcoal gray **Harker Building** (No. 728) may catch your eye: *"Je ne veux pas travailler"* ("I don't want to

work"). Of course, this refers to the famous Portland band Pink Martini and its band leader, Thomas Lauderdale, who has lived here since 1996.

OREGON MUSEUM OF SCIENCE AND INDUSTRY (OMSI)★★

D6–7 1945 SE Water St. – ☏ (503) 797 4000 – www.omsi.edu – ✕ ♿ 🅿 – Tue–Sun 9:30am–5:30pm – $14.50 (3–13 years: $9.75).
On the site of a former power plant on the banks of the Willamette is this remarkable glazed brick building (1992, Zimmer Gunsul Frasca), housing the main attraction of Portland's east. This cultural center brings together a host of interactive exhibitions, an IMAX cinema ($7–8.50/ticket) and a planetarium ($6.75).
Exhibitions on the first floor give children the chance to build bridges, launch ships, and design and test planes. Younger kids have the run of a creative playground. Upstairs, the range of activities on offer begins with the **Life Hall**, where a collection of eerily beautiful human embryos illustrate the different stages of prenatal development. The **Turbine Hall** gives visitors the chance to create a flying machine and program a robot.
Moored on the riverbank behind the museum, the diesel-electric **USS Blueback** submarine, built in 1959 and decommissioned in 1990, is open for guided tours ($7.50). You can visit the bridge, torpedo room, officers' and crew's quarters and mess.

PORTLAND AERIAL TRAM★

C7 3303 SW Bond Ave. – www.gobytram.com – Mon–Fri 5:30am–9:30pm, Sat 9am–5pm, Sun inquire for opening hours – Closed public holidays – Round-trip $4.90.
This cable car provides breathtaking views over the city and nearby peaks including Mount Hood. The four-minute ride(rising 500 ft and traveling just over 1/2 mi) connects the banks of the Willamette to the Oregon Health & Science University on Marquam Hill.

OREGON RAIL HERITAGE CENTER

D7 2250 SE Water Ave. – ☏ (503) 233 1156 – www.orhf.org – Thur–Fri 1pm–5pm, weekend noon–5pm – Free.
Highly recommended for train enthusiasts, this small museum tells the tale of the opening of the railway line that brought Portland much of its prosperity from 1850 onwards. The centerpieces of the collection are three old steam locomotives, including a 1905 Baldwin Locomotive.

Eastside★

If you're on a quest to find Portland's green, hipster side, come to the eastern bank of the river. Called Eastside, this area comprises North/Northeast, Southeast and Central Eastside. These districts, more bohemian than the west of Portland, contain a plethora of places to visit, ranging from the most sophisticated to the completely off-the-wall. It's here that most of the 'real' inhabitants of Portland live today, in these peaceful areas, with their sleepy, small village-like atmosphere. Around every corner the windows and terraces pulse with life; a girl lounges in front of an arthouse cinema; the restaurants and cafés are teeming with people. Eastside is simultaneously authentic and hip. In North/Northeast, the Alberta Arts District and Mississippi/Williams have lively nightlife and a strong art scene. In the Southeast, venture into Division/Clinton and Hawthorne/Belmont districts, where third-wave cafés and bars serving natural wine rub shoulders with record stores and tiny boutiques overflowing with charm.

▶ **Access:** Eastside brings together all the districts to the east of the Willamette River. Central Eastside is bordered to the north by Northeast, after East Burnside St., and to the south by Southeast, after SE Hawthorne Blvd. Accessed by bus and tram (lines A and B), these districts are sprawling, and it may be necessary to go by car or take a taxi, particularly when you go out at night.
Area maps pp. 16–17 and p. 37. Detachable map C1–4 DH1–8.
▶ **Tip:** Eastside doesn't have many tourist attractions, but it's ideal for a shopping spree, a foodie dinner or an evening seeing local bands playing the bars.
♿ *Addresses pp. 69, 70, 73, 80, 81, 82, 89, 90, 97 and 98.*

CENTRAL EASTSIDE

D5–6 Founded in 1845, this district soon became the industrial and commercial hub of the city, particularly with the arrival of the railway in 1869. As it developed, its warehouses multiplied. Following a gradual restoration, the old buildings are now home to restaurants, workshops, and stores selling tasty treats and trendy decor. In fact, the culinary revolution that turned Portland into one of the leading lights of the US food scene in the late 2000s all began here. Wander around and take in the striking architecture as well as the stores. You may be lucky enough to come across one of the truly colossal goods trains (sometimes over a mile long!) that still cross the district (watch out when crossing the railway tracks). Here and there you can also spot **murals** that add to Portland's artistic, creative flair. Begin your culinary adventure in Central Eastside, at the end of **Morrison Bridge**, and head up towards Washington Street. You'll reach Grand

© Jamie Francis/Travel Portland

Central Eastside

Avenue before heading down towards Southeast.

The **Weatherley Building** *(516 SE Morrison St.)*, which houses an athletic-wear store on the first floor, is the tallest building in the district. Dating from 1928, this unmistakable building features an arcade of arches set into the gray facade.

ARCHITECTURAL HERITAGE CENTER

D6 701 SE Grand Ave. – 📞 *(503) 231 7264 – visitahc.org – Wed–Sat 10am–5pm – $7.*
Portland became aware of its wealth of architectural heritage in the 1980s, putting an end to decades of 'progressive' demolition. In this restored old house, discover the traces of buildings that have now disappeared. Above all, take a look at the temporary exhibitions on topics linked to architecture or on architects who have made their mark on the city. AHC also organizes guided tours of various districts (♿ *p. 120*).

SOUTHEAST

DH6–8 The bohemian Southeast is home to foodie establishments, a vibrant nightlife, and myriad fascinating vintage stores. As it's fairly spread out, the district is more easily accessed by car, but if you do walk or ride a bike, enjoy losing yourself in the streets and avenues that are alternately bustling and calm. There, you'll see many typical Portland houses from the early 1900s and 1930s.

Start off by making for **Division Street**, a thoroughfare particularly beloved by gastronomes. At the top of the street, between 9th and 10th Avenues, is the latest and already iconic mural by the Irish artist **Fin Dac**, which depicts a stunning, mysterious woman whose abundant hair is actually made of plants.

To the north of Division, around **Ladd Circle**, a large circular open space covered in grass, you'll find a residential neighborhood with meticulously plotted geometric avenues. This was one of Portland's first attempts at urban planning, led by 1850s mayor William Sargent Ladd.

National Hat Museum★ – *E6 – 1928 SE Ladd Ave. – ☏ (503) 319 0799 – www. thehatmuseum.com – Guided tours 1:30pm, booking required by phone or online (up to 5 people) – $35.*

Built in the early 1900s, this historic house contains an incredible collection of hats. Started in the early 20th century by Rebecca Reingold, a milliner and the house's first owner, it was then taken over by eccentric novelist Alyce Cornyn-Selby, who added hundreds of hats to the collection, each bigger, rarer or more astonishing than the next. Today, it is Lu Ann Trotebas, dressed as an elegant lady from the Belle Époque (sporting a hat to complete the look, of course), who guides visitors through the galleries of hats. Trotebas takes you on a trip back through several centuries of fascinating history, from Amish hats and 1950s creations by the famous French-American milliner Lilly Daché, to military caps and baseball hats.

By continuing your walk north you'll come across **Hawthorne Boulevard**, a long, bustling artery with many shops. It's more popular towards the Mount Tabor end. **Southeast Belmont Street** also shouldn't be missed if you want to get an idea of the eccentric population that lives here. From the wild video games room of the arcade overrun by children and adults pining for the eighties, to the cult café set in a dilapidated Victorian house, to the dark bars with their grungy musicians in worn leather, soak up the spirit of eccentric Portland.

Even farther north, the **Laurelhurst** district around Coe Square features a gilded statue of Joan of Arc (a replica of the one on Place des Pyramides in Paris) and undulating, chic, tree-lined streets with beautiful homes.

MOUNT TABOR PARK★

GH6–7 Accessed by car or on foot for the more adventurous *(around 1hr20min from Hawthorne Bridge)*, while biking is slightly quicker *(around 35min)*. This is one of the city's major parks, covering slopes of a small extinct volcano (about 630 ft tall). You can still see the dark cinders of the former caldera, which has been turned into an amphitheater. Numerous paths lined by tall pine trees lead to the top, where there is a spectacular **panoramic view★★** over the city and Mount Hood (☏ *p. 52*). It's particularly breathtaking at sunset. This park also has large reservoirs, with various trails weaving between them.

43

Trail Blazers and Timbers, pride of the city

*Located in Lloyd District, the **Moda Center** (1 N Center Ct St. – nbatickets.nba.com) is home to the **Portland Trail Blazers (the Blazers)**, Portland's NBA team. It's well worth going to a game, even if you just go to soak up the atmosphere. It's more than just a game: in a spectacular show, cheerleaders entertain the spectators (over 20,000 per game) during lulls and at half-time. And, of course, the food stalls in the stadium sell great bites. While the **Portland Timbers** aren't the best-known pro soccer team, they're still intriguing and impressive for the enthusiasm of their fans, fervor unmatched on this side of the Atlantic. Over 21,000 soccer fans attend each home game at **Providence Park** (1844 SW Morrison St. – www.mlssoccer.com/tickets), west of Downtown. There's such demand that the stadium was recently expanded. The Timbers Army, the most enthusiastic fans, are in charge of ensuring a lively atmosphere.*

NORTH/NORTHEAST

Lloyd

D4–5 Just across from Old Town is this very lively area housing the Convention Center, the **Moda Center** for concerts and sports events and the Lloyd Center (👆 p. 90), the biggest shopping center in Portland. From its streets and some of its hotels and bars, you can enjoy great views over the river and city skyline.

44

Mississippi/Williams

CD2 **North Mississippi Avenue** used to be composed of buildings with crumbling facades until a successful restoration turned it into a hotspot for hipsters. The street, with its quirky boutiques and dining establishments, is typical of the eastern districts of the city: young people ride past on their bikes in outfits that could be featured in fashion magazines, freelancers tap away at their laptops in cafés with neo-industrial decor (rough-hewn wooden tables, exposed pipes, bare walls), and stalls sell second-hand clothes to Portlanders wearing flannel shirts, sporting full beards and with their tattoos proudly on show.

Alberta Arts District

CE1 You'll find a similar atmosphere on **Northeast Alberta Street**, a calm district with quaint houses surrounded by bustling art galleries, independent stores, cafés and restaurants. Colorful murals plaster the walls.

© NBAE/Travel Portland

Portland Trail Blazers at Moda Center

Outside the City Center

Head just a few miles out of the city center and you'll start to see how Portland's urban planning is unique in the US. The gray concrete disappears and suddenly you're surrounded by woodlands and greenery. Take a break from the (relative) frenzy of the central districts and soak up the tranquility of gardens, parks, forests and lakes—within easy reach of central Portland.

▶ **Access:** Indicated for each attraction.
Area map p. 37. Surrounding area map pp. 50–51.

ELK ROCK GARDEN (BISHOP'S CLOSE)★

Map I 6 miles south of the city center on SW Macadam Ave. SW Military Lane – ℘ (503) 636 5613 – www. elkrockgarden.org – 8am–5pm – Free – buses 35, 36 to SW Riverside/Military. In 1916 rich grain merchant Peter Kerr built a Scottish-style manor house on a cliff. Around the house he planted an English garden, designed by John Olmsted, incorporating plants from his trips around the world. Today, the house and gardens belong to the Episcopal Church.

LEWIS AND CLARK COLLEGE★★

Surrounding area map B2 5.6 miles south of Downtown, on SW Market St. and the I-5 S. 0615 SW Palatine Hill Road – www.lclark.edu – bus no. 39 to L&C Campus & Templeton Student Center. Perched above the city, this vas, old manor, built in 1924 for **Lloyd Frank**, owner of the Meier & Frank department stores, is now part of the prestigious Lewis and Clark College, whose buildings are pleasantly nestled amongst the greenery. The Art Deco-style **gardens** beneath the sumptuous house descend over a gentle slope split into tiers. They are among the most beautiful gardens in Oregon. The view over the large lake and towards Mount Hood, surrounded by different varieties of flowers, topiaries, trees and pines, is simply magnificent.

ST. JOHNS BRIDGE★ AND CATHEDRAL PARK

Surrounding area map B2 9 miles north of Downtown on US 30 W – buses no. 11 or 16 at N Ivanhoe/Leavitt and no. 4 at N Syracuse/Chicago. Moving downstream towards the confluence of the Willamette and Columbia Rivers, there is a large industrial area next to the port on both sides of the river. Among the buildings on the left bank of the river is the huge Montgomery Park warehouse, which was built in 1920.
St. Johns Bridge★ is the tallest bridge in Portland. It was built between 1929 and 1931, in the midst of the Great Depression, providing jobs for hundreds of Portlanders. Its two steel

PDX, the well-loved airport with the cult carpet

PDX is consistently named the best airport in the US, and for good reason: it overflows with top-notch restaurants, local breweries and third-wave coffee shops. It's safe, relaxed and well-equipped, and since there are hardly any lines you can pass through security in mere minutes. Since 1983, its carpet—a green reminiscent of Oregon's natural surroundings, decorated with a geometric pattern that provides an abstract representation of the air traffic controllers' view from their tower—has marked visitors' arrival in a town where everything is done differently. In 2015, the replacement of this carpet with one with a slightly more modern pattern caused an uproar on social media, bringing the PDX cult to fever pitch. Reproduced on socks, T-shirts and bike helmets, the pattern of the old carpet was seen everywhere. Today, Portlanders seem to have gotten used to the new carpet, which, quite rightly, still signals your arrival in the weirdest city in the US!

towers soar 400 ft above the river. Its slender silhouette is best appreciated from **Cathedral Park** *(5am–midnight)* where you can wander between the concrete bridge supports, with the pointed arches making you feel as though you're in a Gothic cathedral.

THE GROTTO ★

Surrounding area map C2 *9 miles east of Downtown on the I-84 E. 8840 NE Skidmore St. – ℘ (503) 254 7371 – www.thegrotto.org – 9am–6:30pm – Access to the Upper Gardens $7.50 – bus no. 12 at Northeast Sandy/Grotto, no. 71 at NE Prescott/85th, and 72 or 272 at NE 82nd/Sandy.*

This small, eccentric park, simultaneously peaceful and luxurious, is well worth a visit. When he was a young boy, the pastor Ambrose Mayer promised to dedicate a monument to the Virgin Mary if she saved the life of his mother, who was dying in childbirth. The miracle was granted; his mother was saved. In 1923, Father Mayer, remembering his promise, bought a former quarry from the Union Pacific Railroad Company to turn into a sanctuary.

The enormous artificial grotto has upper contemplative gardens dotted with exotic chapels, statues of saints and even a mystical labyrinth. From the glass-fronted Marylin Moyer chapel, there is a fantastic vista of the flat-topped Mount St. Helens.

Around Portland

A favored playground for Portlanders who can escape the city for a weekend's camping or outdoor activities, the areas surrounding the city have many delights in store, including the majestic Mount Hood, whose conical form brings to mind Japan's Mount Fuji; the vineyards of the Willamette and Tualatin Valleys, which do a fine job of showcasing the best qualities of the pinot noir; and a fantastic aviation museum.

▶ **Access:** Indicated for each attraction. A car is a must unless joining a tour. (♿ *p. 118*).
Surrounding area map pp. 50–51.
♿ *Addresses pp. 75, 76, 84, 98 and 99.*

COLUMBIA RIVER GORGE NATIONAL SCENIC AREA★★

Surrounding area map CD2
On I-84, from Troutdale (16 miles east of Portland) to The Dalles (81 miles east of Portland). 🛈 ☎ *(541) 386 8758 – www.fs.usda.gov/crgnsa.*
Stretching from Portland's suburbs to the mouth of the Deschutes River, the Columbia River Gorge Scenic Area (170 sq miles) contains over 90 waterfalls, as well as national parks and cliffs that soar to over 650 ft. The incredible panoramic views from the top shouldn't be missed. The second longest river in the US, Columbia River forges its way through volcanic basalt following the state border between Oregon and Washington. Sadly, a terrible fire in 2017 ravaged the cliffs above the waterfalls, but this hasn't completely altered the majestic beauty of this place.
The **Historic Columbia River Highway★★** *(US 30)* is an alternative route to I-84, passing through spectacular landscapes. Finished in 1915, there are two sections of the highway, linked by I-84: 21.2 miles between Troutdale *(exit 17)* and Ainsworth State Park *(exit 40),* and 15.4 miles between Mosier *(exit 69)* and The Dalles *(exit 84).* Catch the most stunning views at **Portland Women's Forum State Park★★★** *(mile 10)* and **Crown Point★★** *(mile 11)* at Vista House, where the visitor center and dome are worth visiting *(www. vistahouse.com).* The gorge has some spectacular waterfalls, particularly **Latourell Falls★★** *(2.5 miles after Vista House)* where you can get extremely close to the thin, powerful cascade of water that falls some 260 ft, and above all **Multnomah Falls★★** *(I-84, exit 31),* which are 6201 ft high. Take one of the footpaths that scales the cliffs and you can enjoy a breathtaking bird's eye view over the falls.
Hood River is a small and trendy historic town that makes a great base from which to explore the gorges.

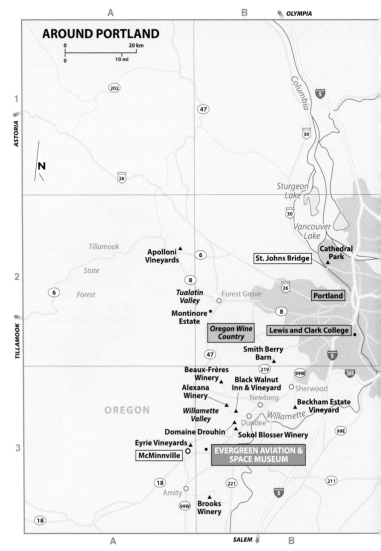

AROUND PORTLAND

OLYMPIA

ASTORIA

TILLAMOOK

50

SALEM

0   20 km
0   10 mi

N

202

47

30

Columbia

5

26

30

Sturgeon Lake

Vancouver Lake

Tillamook

State

Forest

6

Apolloni Vineyards

6

8

Tualatin Valley

Forest Grove

Montinore Estate

Oregon Wine Country

47

Smith Berry Barn

Beaux-Frères Winery

Alexana Winery

Willamette Valley

Domaine Drouhin

Eyrie Vineyards

McMinnville

18

Amity

99W

Brooks Winery

221

18

26

St. Johns Bridge

Cathedral Park

Portland

8

Lewis and Clark College

5

219

Black Walnut Inn & Vineyard

Newberg

99W

205

Sherwood

Beckham Estate Vineyard

Dundee

Willamette

Sokol Blosser Winery

99E

EVERGREEN AVIATION & SPACE MUSEUM

211

5

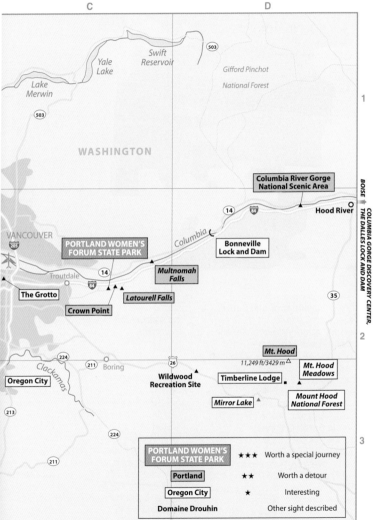

C

D

Yale
Lake

Swift
Reservoir

503

Gifford Pinchot

National Forest

Lake
Merwin

503

1

WASHINGTON

**Columbia River Gorge
National Scenic Area**

14 I-84 Hood River

BOISE →

COLUMBIA GORGE DISCOVERY CENTER,
THE DALLES LOCK AND DAM

VANCOUVER
I-205

**PORTLAND WOMEN'S
FORUM STATE PARK**

Columbia

**Bonneville
Lock and Dam**

Troutdale 14 I-84

*Multnomah
Falls*

51

The Grotto

Latourell Falls

Crown Point

35

2

224 211 Boring

26

Mt. Hood

11,249 ft/3429 m △ *Mt. Hood
Meadows*

Oregon City

Clackamas

**Wildwood
Recreation Site**

Timberline Lodge ■

Mirror Lake ▲

*Mount Hood
National Forest*

213

224

211

3

**PORTLAND WOMEN'S
FORUM STATE PARK** ★★★ Worth a special journey

Portland ★★ Worth a detour

Oregon City ★ Interesting

Domaine Drouhin Other sight described

C

D

© 4nadia/iStockphoto.com

Crown Point, Columbia River Gorge National Scenic Area

At the **Bonneville Lock and Dam★** *(I-84, exit 40 – ☎ 541-374 8820 – www. nwp.usace.army.mil/bonneville)* and **The Dalles Lock and Dam★** *(I-84, exit 87 – ☎ 541-296 9778 – www.nwp. usace.army.mil/The-Dalles)* visitor centers, which are managed by the US Army Corps of Engineers, you can learn how the river has been managed and used, and also see migrating fish. **Columbia Gorge Discovery Center★★** *– 5000 Discovery Dr. – The Dalles – ☎ 541-296 8600 – www. gorgediscovery.org – 9am–5pm – closed Thanksgiving, 25 Dec and 1 Jan – $9 (under 17s: $5).* Interactive exhibits let visitors discover the tremendous eruptions and floods that sculpted the gorge, as well as Lewis and Clark's

journey down the Columbia River. The **Ice Age Exhibit** includes a life-size mammoth.

AROUND MOUNT HOOD★★

Surrounding area map D3 On US 26, 50 miles east of Portland. 🚹 *☎ (503) 622 3017 – www.mthoodterritory.com and www.mthoodchamber.com.*
The snow-topped peak of Mount Hood, Oregon's highest point, rises 11,249 feet above sea level. In 1805, the explorers Lewis and Clark *(👤 p. 126)* were the first white Americans to set eyes on this volcanic cone, which was named by British sailors. In the mid-19th century, the sight of Mount Hood signaled the end of the long journey

to Oregon for thousands of exhausted pioneers.

Tourists can take a walk along the forest trails, admire the alpine glaciers and drive the picturesque roads, stopping along the way in rustic guesthouses and skiing the challenging slopes, open all year round. Soon after leaving Portland, you pass through the small town of **Boring**. Its inhabitants clearly have a good sense of humor, because a sign advertises the fact that its sister cities are Dull in Scotland and Bland in Australia!

Before reaching Mount Hood, make sure you stop off at **Wildwood Recreation Forest Site** *(65670 US 26, Welches – www.blm.gov/visit/ wildwood-recreation-site – $5/vehicle)*. Here you can dive into lush, relatively untouched nature, walking boardwalks over the turbulent waters of the Salmon River and taking a five-mile interpretive trail through the forest. Twenty miles to the east, **Timberline Lodge★** *(on US 26, 6 miles north of Government Camp –* 🕭 *p. 98)*, which was built in 1936–37 and inaugurated by President Roosevelt, boasts fine examples of US artisan furnishings, including carved wood, marquetry and stained glass. A particularly outstanding feature of this luxurious historical building is the large lounge with its central chimney. Most of the decoration was made with materials salvaged from the area. Film buffs will recognize the lodge because the outside scenes of *The Shining* were shot here!

From here, walkers can tackle the picturesque 40-mile **Timberline Trail★★** *(www.oregonhikers.org)*,

discovering striking mountain landscapes. A recommended season for hiking is at the end of summer when the trail conditions are at their best.

From Government Camp, head for the Mirror Lake Trailhead parking lot *(don't leave anything out in your car, it may get broken into)* to set out on the lovely **Mirror Lake★** trail (an easy 2hr30min round trip). The route climbs up through the forest, where you can truly appreciate Oregon's wealth of biodiversity and see some remarkable trees with bent trunks which would have been used by the Native Americans as landmarks. Some of the trees are hundreds of years old. From the lake, the **view★★** of Mount Hood and its perfect reflection in the water is beautiful, particularly in the early morning.

With its high meadows, **Mount Hood Meadows** ski station★ *(on the US 35, 9.6 miles north of Government Camp –* 🕿 *503-337 2222 – www.skihood.com)* is one of the best places to ski in the Northwest. The ski lifts take you to the highest point of 7,300 feet, giving you breathtaking views over the other volcanoes in the range.

OREGON CITY★

***Surrounding area map C3** On Route 99E, 11.5 miles south of Portland on I-205.* 🖪 🕿 *(503) 656 1619 – www.oregoncity.org.*

Founded in 1844 at the end of the 2,170 mile **Oregon Trail**, this former industrial city of 36,000 inhabitants was the first village of the Willamette Valley and the first capital of the

Oregon Territory. Surrounded by forests and bordered by the Willamette River and its waterfalls, Oregon City is a small city with a pleasant atmosphere and plenty of cafés, craft breweries, etc.

End of the Oregon Trail Interpretive Center★ – *1726 Washington St. – ☏ (503) 657 9336 – www.historic oregoncity.org – ♿ 🅿 – Mon-Sat 9:30am–5pm, Sun 10:30am–5pm – $13 (4-12 years: $7, 13–18 years: $9).* This center is housed in three 50-foot-tall buildings shaped like covered wagons and set in the 8 acres of Abernathy Green, the end of the Oregon Trail. Guides in period dress describe the six-month-long journey taken by pioneers, and a video retraces the (fictional) lives of three migrants.

54

OREGON WINE COUNTRY ★★

Willamette Valley

Surrounding area map B3 *On Route 99W west of I-5, from 20 to 40 miles southwest of Portland. Between Newberg and Lafayette, small roads stem from Route 99W to plunge deeper into the vineyards and towards the wineries. 🔋 ☏ 866 548 5018 – www.oregonwinecountry.org.*

🐦 The best base camps for exploring the area are Newberg, Dundee and McMinnville. The Wheatland Ferry *(toll)* allows you to cross the Willamette from the Amity region and rejoin I-5, which connects Portland to the south of Oregon.

Over the years, the **northern Willamette valley**—located at the same latitude as Burgundy, France —has become one of the leading regions in the wine world (despite relatively little publicity), with over 500 wineries. Most of these are small, family-run businesses, which are often open to the public for visits and wine tastings *(for a fee)*. Willamette Valley has **seven wine-growing regions** (the winemakers call these AVAs: American Viticultural Areas). The wineries are most highly concentrated on the gentle slopes of the Dundee Hills, Yamhill Carlton and the Chehalem Mountains. Around Amity and McMinnville, the vineyards become steeper, with landscapes that evoke Tuscany, Burgundy or the Garonne valley (according to preference). Here, in fine weather, you can catch incredible views of the Cascade volcanic range.

The region's bright and lively wines are characterized by their subtle aromas and low alcohol content. Established in the 1960s, Oregon's wine industry was barely known to the public until, in 1979, the unthinkable happened: a pinot noir from Eyrie Vineyards (🐦 *p. 60*) ranked first in a French wine tasting, coming ahead of a number of highly acclaimed French wines! Exceptional terroirs and a long growing season with a dry summer, cool fall and wet winter, tempered by the proximity to the ocean, create ideal conditions. These are not only perfect for pinot noir, but also for other varieties like chardonnay, merlot, cabernet sauvignon and pinot gris. The almost-deserted countryside roads are lined with vineyards, orchards and sales stands. Often the vineyards are hidden by pine forests that create a natural barrier, favoring an optimal

development of the vine. Many winemakers use organic practices to make their wines.

Black Walnut Inn and Vineyard – *From Dundee, head towards Lafayette, turn right onto SW 9th St., then continue on NE Worden Hill Rd; the winery is located on the right –* ℘ (503) 538 8663 – www.blackwalnut-inn.com – *Wine tasting: flight of 6 wines with appetizers (1hr) Thur-Sun 11:30am, 1:30pm and 3pm – $65*. This winery is sure to please. An imposing Tuscan-style property looks out over the 15 acres of vines carpeting the hills, providing great views across the valley. Here, they bring out the best in pinots gris and noir *(around $35)*, as well as chardonnay.

Continue along NE Worden Hill Rd and the Alexana Winery is on your left.

Alexana Winery – ℘ (503) 537 3100 – www.alexanawinery.com – *Wine tasting 11am–5pm (10am–4pm in winter) – $25*. Spread over 80 acres, the varieties grown here are chardonnay *($65/bottle)* and pinot noir *($55–85/bottle)*. While the riesling gives off a lovely freshness (white peach, lemon and jasmine aromas), the chardonnay is characterized at first by its bright flavor, which is then counterbalanced by a long, full-bodied aftertaste and plenty of minerality. As for the pinots, they excel; get a sense of the full range of flavors this variety can offer.

Domaine Drouhin – *From Dundee, head towards McMinnville and take the first small road, McDougal, off to the right, then immediately turn right onto Breyman Orchards Road* – ℘ (503) 864 2700 – www.

domainedrouhin.com – *Wine tastings (flight of 5): 11am–4pm – $25*. This 225-acre winery is one of the region's best known. It's managed by Véronique Drouhin, who also holds the reins of the renowned Burgundy winery of the same name, alongside her three brothers. In 2014, the family acquired Roserock Vineyards (275 acres), making this family, with its Burgundy roots, one of the leading producers of pinot in Oregon. The pinot noirs, with their blackcurrant and raspberry aromas, faintly spicy and smoky, are in keeping with traditional Burgundian style while also adapting to the geographical characteristics of the Willamette Valley *(from $35/bottle)*. White wine fans will enjoy the chardonnay *($35/bottle)* and pinot gris.

Sokol Blosser Winery – *From Dundee, head towards McMinnville. After 2 miles take Sokol Blosser Lane on your right –* ℘ (503) 864 2282 – www.sokolblosser.com – *Wine tastings: daily 10am–4pm – From $20*. This winery has a splendid wine tasting room, with untreated wood and large windows, and a terrace with views over the winery's 100 acres of local vineyards. You can try pinot gris *(around $25/bottle)*, pinot noir rosé *($25/bottle)* and pinot noir *($40–80/bottle)*. Other varieties are also represented, such as chardonnay and sangiovese. Noteworthy are the pinot noirs, with their soft tannins, delicately spiced cherry, blackcurrant and toasted bread aromas, and lovely lingering aftertaste.

Brooks Winery – *14 miles southeast of McMinnville on Route 99W, then Route 153 – 21101 SE Cherry Blossom*

56

Lane – Amity – ✆ *(503) 435 1278* – *www.brookswine.com* – *11am–5pm.* Since 1998, this winery founded by Jimi Brooks has adopted biodynamic cultivation as its guiding principle. Set in a magnificent location opposite the Cascades, the wine cellar is equipped with a fantastic wine tasting area where you can have lunch while gazing out over a pretty flower garden and rows of expertly pruned vines. While the pinot noir reigns king *($25–60/ bottle)*, you can also taste delicious rieslings here *(around $25/bottle)*, as well as fortified wines that go wonderfully with dessert.

Beckham Estate Vineyard – *7.8 miles east of Newberg on Route 99W – 30790 SW Heater Rd – Sherwood –* ✆ *(971) 645 3466 – beckhamestatevineyard.com – Mar–Oct: Fri–Sun 11am–5pm; Nov–Feb: Sat noon–4pm and by appointment.* This vineyard at the top of Mount Perham was sculpted by Andrew and Annedria Beckham, who pulled up trees themselves to adapt this unusual property. Andrew, an arts professor, is also the only winemaker in Willamette Valley to make his own amphorae in which he ages some of his wines. This makes the visit and wine tasting even more fascinating. Pinot noir *($30–60/bottle)*, red or rosé, and riesling *($24/bottle)* are the main varieties grown here.

Beaux-Frères Winery – *7.7 miles to the west of Newberg on Route 240 – 15155 NE North Valley Rd – Newberg –* ✆ *(503) 537 1137 – www.beauxfreres. com – By appointment.* Don't try to catch a glimpse of the vines from the road, because they are well hidden up on the higher ground. Since 1990, the pinot noir produced here has acquired fans around the world *($75–85/ bottle)*. Extremely authentic, this winery takes a lot from the personality of its owner Michael Etzel, as well as the techniques used, which all center around biodynamic cultivation and are in perfect harmony with the landscape.

Tualatin Valley

Surrounding area map AB2 *By Route 26W around 26 miles west of Portland.* 🖪 *www.oregonwinecountry.org.* ⊘ The best base camp for exploring the area is Forest Grove. Oregon Helicopters, a company based out of Hillsboro airport, organizes rides that give an overview of the geography of the Tualatin Valley *(oregonhelicopters.com).* This fertile valley is known as 'Portland's garden.' Many restaurants in the city source products for their menus here, such as lamb, strawberries, raspberries and assorted vegetables. At many of the farms, like **Smith Berry Barn** *(24500 SW Scholls Ferry Road Hillsboro –* ✆ *503-628 2172 – smithberrybarn.com – Tue–Sun 10am–5pm)*, visitors can pick their own fruit to take home with them. This region is also known for being a favorite with big companies. The valley is home to Nike and Intel, to name only a few. Nicknamed the Silicon Forest, the Tualatin Valley has a population of nearly 600,000 people living in 13 different towns. Lastly, the valley has some of the most interesting wine production in the Portland area.

Montinore Estate – *3 miles south of Forest Grove – 3663 SW Dilley Rd*

– ☎ (503) 359 5012 – www.montinore. com – Wine tastings 11am–5pm – 3 glasses $15. A pioneer in the region for biodynamic wines, Montinore's vines cover over 197 acres. The high-quality wines produced in this winery—which has an elegant tasting room—showcase the finest nuances of pinot noir in a number of different vintages *(around $50/bottle).* Cataclysm, for instance, stands out for the toasted and delicate aromas of wild strawberries with a lovely long aftertaste, while Graham's Block 7 has notes of intense dark fruits, leather and chocolate. The same spectrum can be found in the riesling and pinot gris.

Apolloni Vineyard *– 9.5 miles northwest of Forest Grove on Route 8W – 14135 NW Timmerman Rd – ☎ (503) 359 3606 – apolloni.com – Wine tastings 11am–5pm – 3 glasses $15/20.* The atmosphere and setting are more bucolic and rustic here than at Montinore. There is a wide range of varieties on offer, including sangiovese and nebbiolo, which are hard to find in this region, and which reflect the owners' Italian roots. Highly recommended are the pinot gris *($18/bottle),* with its pear aromas, minerality and citrus finish, and the Feminia pinot noir *($20–35/bottle),* which varies a great deal depending on the vintage, but is a wonderfully elegant wine.

MCMINNVILLE★

Surrounding area map A3 *On Route 99W, 41.5 miles south of Portland.* 🚹 *417 NW Adams St. (between 4th and 5th St.) – ☎ (503) 472 6196 – 8am–5pm (closed at lunchtime) – visitmcminnville.com.* The capital of Yamhill County is at the heart of the **wine-growing area** of the northern Willamette Valley. The town makes an ideal base camp to explore the area, featuring a well-preserved historic town center full of 19th-century buildings that now house cafés, restaurants and little antique shops. Leaving McMinnville, small country roads lead to dozens of farms and wineries, spread out across the wooded hillsides covered in oaks.

Eyrie Vineyards *– 935 E 10th Ave. – ☎ (503) 472 6315 – www.eyrie vineyards.com – Wine tastings: daily noon–5pm – $15 (4 wines), $25 (7 wines).* This 60-acre winery has a special place in Oregon's winemaking history; one of its pinot noirs paved the way for local winemakers on the world stage. The winery continues to produce excellent vintages, from faintly smoky but refreshing pinot gris *($18.50/bottle)* to outstanding pinot noir *($37.50–$80/bottle).* And don't forget about the chardonnay, chasselas, muscat and melon varieties.

EVERGREEN AVIATION & SPACE MUSEUM★★★

Surrounding area map B3 *3.5 miles south of McMinnville. Leave the town on SE 3 Mile Lane, which continues from NE 3rd St., then turn left onto US 18. The museum will be on your left. 500 NE Capt. Michael King Smith Way – ☎ (503) 434 4180 – www. evergreenmuseum.org – 9am–5pm – $27 (under 17s: $19), includes entry to the aviation museum, the space*

Spruce Goose, Evergreen Aviation & Space Museum

museum and one ticket for the IMAX theater; water park: $20/29, check website for opening hours.

Set aside at least three hours to visit this huge complex with its multiple zones. As well as the two exhibition hangars, there is an IMAX theater and a water park with ten waterslides. Among the 200 models on display in the hangar dedicated to the **history of aviation** is the largest wooden airplane ever constructed, the billionaire Howard Hughes's legendary Spruce Goose (1947). This "monster," whose structure was made from wood because of metal scarcity at the time, represents the wild dream of a man who wanted to conquer the skies.

Unfortunately, his project only flew once, for one minute, over a mile, and just 70 feet up! Another exhibit of note is the first ever flying machine, created in 1903. The man who launched it flew seated for 12 seconds at 120 feet of altitude, and at a speed of 27 mph. In the second hangar, dedicated to the **history of space exploration**, information panels, photos and videos recount the relentless struggle between the US and the USSR to prove their superiority and control of space during the Cold War. Fans will enjoy retrospectives on the space missions as well as the rockets, satellites and other missiles that are on display.

OREGON COAST ★★★

Off map While temperatures are always mild (50–70°F on average), many say that September is the best month for a trip to the coast. In summer, the weather is particularly unpredictable, changing suddenly from sun to fog. High season also brings hordes of tourists and a fair share of traffic jams. US 101 is the main highway that follows the coastline.

Astoria★

At the junction of US 26, US 30 and US 101, 96 miles northwest of Portland. 🗗 *111 W. Marine Dr. – ☎ (503) 325 6311 – www.oldoregon.com and www.travelastoria.com – Mon–Sat 9am–5pm, Sun 10am–5pm.*

A former fur trading post founded in 1811, Astoria was the first US settlement west of the Rocky Mountains. A flourishing haven at the mouth of the Columbia in the 1850s, it's still an active harbor town of around 9,500 inhabitants, despite the gradual decline of local industry, centered around salmon fishing and timber. With its steep streets, colorful hillside Victorian houses, enormous bridge spanning the river estuary and easy-going way of life, Astoria's nickname is 'Little San Francisco'. The city is also known for being the setting of the cult film *The Goonies*. The **Riverwalk**★ is a pleasant path that follows the river for over six miles, with options of walking, biking or hopping on the **Astoria Riverfront Trolley** *(50min round trip – this small train departs every hour – $1)*. Those who want to explore the river estuary and its wildlife can set sail with

Columbia River Eco Tours *(W. Mooring Basin Slip D-5 – ☎ 503-468 9197 – columbiariverecotours.com – 2hr $95, 3hr $125, 4hr $150).*

Columbia River Maritime Museum★★ – *On the Riverwalk – 792 Marine Dr. – ☎ (503) 325 2323 – www.crmm.org – 9:30am–5pm – $14.* This fascinating museum illustrates the region's long maritime tradition, from Native American canoes to the coastguard and fearless rescuers that monitor the formidable Columbia River mouth. Indeed, the estuary is littered with hundreds of wrecks because of a devastating tidal bore, the monstrous waves of which can reach heights of close to 40 ft in storms.

Heritage Museum – *On the corner of 16th St. and Exchange St. – May–Sept: 10am–5pm; Oct–Apr: Tue–Sat 11am–4pm – $4.* Discover this museum's collection of Indian baskets and a partially reconstructed old Astoria saloon, all housed in the former city hall.

Flavel House – *441 8th St. – May–Sept: 10am–5pm; Oct–Apr: 10am–5pm; $6.* This Queen Anne-style house (1886) still has its original furnishings. History buffs will enjoy the Clatsop County Historical Society tour *(☎ 503-325 2203 – www.cumtux.org).*

Astoria Column– *To the south of the city – www.astoriacolumn.org – From sunrise to sunset – Free – 🅿 $5.* Modeled on Trajan's Column in Rome, it has stood on this 600-foot hill since 1926. Climb the 164 steps to the top to catch stunning views over the ocean and to the west over the **Astoria-Megler Bridge**, the world's longest truss bridge.

Whale watching

In the 19th century, gray whales faced extinction because of overfishing, but today more than 18,000 of them pass close to the Oregon coast in winter and spring as they embark on their 7,000-mile journey between the Bering Sea and Mexico. In the large cities along the coast, tourist agencies organize trips to provide a closer view. When the sea is calm, you can catch sight of the 13-foot-high blows of the whales that surface from various spots along the headlands. From Christmas to late March, tens of thousands of whale watchers go up and down the coastline, looking for the best viewing points. When there are enough whales passing by, they're even visible from the mainland.

Fort Clatsop National Memorial★★ – *6 miles southwest of the US 101 - 92343 Fort Clatsop Rd – ℘ (503) 861 2471 – www.nps.gov/lewi – From early Sept to late June: 9am–5pm; rest of the year: 9am–4pm – $7 (under 16s: free).* In 1805, President Thomas Jefferson sent William Clark and Meriwether Lewis to explore the Louisiana Purchase. Near the location of present-day Astoria, they established an encampment which they named Fort Clatsop after a local Indian tribe. The fort was built on the encampment where Lewis and Clark's exhibition spent the winter of 1805–06 and is a replica of the original camp. The scents of smoked meat, dried furs and wet wood evoke this great adventure. Despite a "wet, cold and disagreeable" winter, on seeing the Pacific coast they wrote in their journals, "Ocean in view! O! The joy!" Make sure you don't miss the movie *A Clatsop Winter Story* and the items that are on show, including a 1795 musket, a bearskin quiver and replicas of the diaries kept by the explorers.

Cannon Beach★★

On US 101, 22 miles south of Astoria and 80 miles west of Portland. ▯ 207 N. Spruce St. – ℘ (503) 436 2623 – www.cannon beach.org. This little town of 1,700 inhabitants owes its charm to the long gracious arc of its **sandy beach**. It has attracted a colony of artists, who in turn have attracted well-off travelers. **Haystack Rock★★** is a colossal basalt sea stack shaped by erosion that rises 235 ft out of the water and is a nesting site for many sea birds.

Ecola State Park★★★ – *US 101, 2 miles north of Cannon Beach – ℘ (503) 436 2844 – www.oregonstateparks.org – $5/car.* This park provides a **scenic overlook★★★** over nine miles of lush forest and coastline described by Lewis and Clark. The hiking trails, a number of which pass through the dense forests, include an eight-mile section of the **Oregon Coast Trail**. Indian Beach is the starting point of a one-mile nature trail. The park is popular for its whale watching spots, for surfing and **beachcombing**.

Addresses

Clyde Common
© Ludovic Maisant/hemis.fr

🍴 *Where to eat*

Portland's food scene is booming, and the city benefits from many top restaurants, proximity to organic and sustainable agriculture, and more than 600 **food carts**. From these you can try cuisines from around the world, on the go and on the cheap, particularly at lunchtime. In the evening, make the most of **happy hour**, between around 4:30pm and 6:30pm: a shortened menu gives you the chance to dine at a trendy restaurant for half the price. Downtown, the Pearl District and Northwest 23rd Ave. are chicer and more expensive, while the more alternative, imaginative restaurants can be found on the Eastside.

🕯 *Meals, p. 112.*

🕯 *Find the addresses on our maps using the number in the listing (for example ①). The coordinates in red (for example C2) refer to the detachable map (inside the cover).*

DOWNTOWN

Area map pp. 16–17

$15–30

⓫ **Bombay Chaat House** – *C5* – *804 SW 12th Ave. – ☎ (503) 241 7944 – www.bombaychaathouse.org – 10:30am–6pm (5:30pm Sat) – Closed Sun – $4/8.* This food cart serves authentic vegetarian and vegan Indian cuisine, bursting with spices that warm your body and soul in the Portland rain. The tandoori naan breads and lentil and chickpea curries are simply divine, while experiments in fusion cuisine, like the falafel burgers with turmeric or masala fries with tamarind chutney are a great success.

㊱ **Maurice** – *C5* – *921 SW Oak St. – ☎ (503) 224 9921 – www.mauricepdx.com – 10am–4pm – Closed Mon.* For a peaceful and healthy break in the beating heart of Downtown, head to this postage stamp-sized restaurant (only open for breakfast and lunch), where Kristen D. Murray serves up simple, tasty dishes using organic ingredients. Indulge in one of her delicious pastries, crème brûlée with a twist or cheesecake to die for.

⑦ **Mother's Bistro & Bar** – *C5* – *121 SW 3rd Ave. – ☎ (503) 464 1122 – www.mothersbistro.com – Tue–Thur 7am–2:30pm, 5:30pm–9pm, Fri 7am–10pm, Sat 8am–10pm, Sun 8am–2:30pm – Closed Mon – $11/25 – Reservations recommended.* Although the dining room is huge, the warm and cozy atmosphere of this restaurant means it's a favorite for couples. The dishes shine in much the same way as the gilded mirrors and crystal chandeliers. This establishment's signature is hearty family food: the chicken and dumplings, meatloaf and gravy and braised pot roast are excellent. It is simply a wonderful restaurant.

$30–50

😊 ② **Bistro Agnes** – *C5* – *527 SW 12th Ave. – ☎ (503) 222 0979 – www.bistroagnes.com – Lunch Mon–Fri 11:30am–2pm, weekend 11am–2pm; dinner 5pm–10pm, Fri–Sat*

5pm–11pm – $22/41. Greg Denton and Gaby Quiñónez Denton, who also own Ox (**&** *p. 74*), have opened this restaurant, revamping the existing the, Super Bite. This is French bistro fare served in a setting to match.

10 **Tasty n Alder** – *C5* – *580 SW 12th Ave.* – *℘ (503) 621 9251 – www. tastynalder.com* – **&** – *9am–2pm, 5:30pm–10pm (11pm Fri–Sat) – $18/64.50.* On the menu at this large, pared-back, neo-industrial space in the heart of Downtown, you'll find Iberian charcuterie, fried oysters, scallops seared to perfection, veal chops and succulent burgers, plus mouth-watering cocktails and a good brunch. It's a place to remember with an eclectic clientèle.

6 **Higgins** – *C6* – *1239 SW Broadway* – *℘ (503) 222 9070 – www.higginsportland.com* – *Lunch: Mon–Fri 11:30am–9:30pm; dinner: Mon–Thur 5pm–9:30pm, Fri–Sat 5pm–10:30pm, Sun 4pm–9:30pm – Entrée $19.50/46.50.* An institution for anyone searching for the delights of Oregon's rich farmland. From duck confit and Dungeness crab to peach clafoutis, local products from nearby farms are turned into sublime dishes. You'll find a nice selection of wines and an elegant, soft-lit atmosphere.

5 **Clyde Common** – *C5* – *1014 SW Harvey Milk St.* – *℘ (503) 228 3333 – www.clydecommon.com* – *Mon–Wed 3pm–11pm, Thur–Fri 3pm–midnight, Sat 10am–midnight, Sun 10am–11pm – $26/32.* Behind its trendy veneer, this Ace Hotel (**&** *Where to stay*) restaurant provides effective cuisine with ingredients from local farms prepared simply. You can also sample

an excellent cocktail or enjoy a cup of coffee during the day.

35 **Headwaters** – *C6* – *1001 SW Broadway* – *At the Heathman Hotel* (**&** *Where to stay*) – *℘ (503) 790 7752 – heathmanhotel.com – Lunch: Mon–Fri 11am–2pm; dinner 5pm–10pm (11pm Fri–Sat).* This vast restaurant with its open kitchen is the domain of one of the most famous chefs in Portland, Vitaly Paley. The menus vary from breakfast to dinner, but whenever you go, delight over oysters from the Oregon coast, delicious crab cakes and the vegetables that are all seasonal. Particularly sublime are the 'made in Oregon' Brussels sprouts, and the strawberries for dessert. There are also very tasty salads served for lunch.

Over $50

25 **Departure** – *C5* – *525 SW Morrison St.* – *15th floor* – *℘ (503) 802 5370 – departureportland.com* – *4pm–11pm, (midnight Fri–Sat) – Menu $50/70.* This Asian-inspired restaurant perches atop hotel The Nines (**&** *Where to stay*) and serves a fine selection of tasty cuisine in a futuristic space evoking an elegant space ship. Unfortunately, the slow service and showy clientèle detract slightly from the exceptional nighttime view of the city lights.

OLD TOWN/CHINATOWN

***Area map** pp. 16–17*

Around $15

12 **Pine Street Market** – *C5* – *126 SW 2nd Ave.* – *www.pinestreetpdx.com* – *9am–10pm – $10/20.* Currently all the

67

🍴

rage, this food court is housed in a building that oozes history. It has been used as a stagecoach storage space, timber warehouse, nightclub and spaghetti factory!

The majestic building, located close to the river, features a number of local purveyors, all under one roof: açai bowls by Kure, Kim Jong Smokehouse's Korean-Texan BBQ, and Teote Outpost's arepas...but also ice cream, ramen, pizza (Checkerboard do one of the best in Portland, topped with garlic and mushrooms) and tacos. There's something for everyone to feast upon at the long communal tables.

$15–30

🌎 **24** **Lovely Rita** – *C5* – *15 NW 4th Ave.* – *☎ (503) 770 0500* – *thehoxton.com/oregon/portland/ hotels* – *7am–11pm (midnight Fri–Sat)* – *$14/30.* Within the elegant Hoxton hotel (*☀ Where to stay),* Lovely Rita offers Mexican-inspired cuisine rooted in the Pacific Northwest. What may seem unlikely on paper proves very convincing on the plate, with grilled octopus, red potatoes, yuzu, black garlic and chipotle. Chic and trendy decor with wooden paneling and leather. Very friendly service.

PEARL DISTRICT

Area map pp. 16–17

Around $15

🌎 **23** **Fuller's** – *C5* – *136 NW 9th Ave.* – *☎ (503) 222 5608* – *www. fullerscoffeeshop.com* – *7am–2pm* – *$7/10.* This is the place for a classic American breakfast. Regulars greet each other over the U-shaped counters, around which aproned waitresses welcome customers, topping up coffees and serving pancakes covered in maple syrup or hash browns with crispy bacon. Forget about your diet and journey back to the 1950s, which can still be found in Pearl District, wedged between a luxury hair salon and two yoga studios.

$30–50

16 **Andina** – *C5*– *1314 NW Glisan St.* – *☎ (503) 228 9535* – *www. andinarestaurant.com* – *11:30am– 2:30pm, 5pm–9:30pm (10:30pm Fri–Sat)* – *$23/40.* The cuisine served in this Peruvian restaurant, a favorite with critics and diners alike, melds South American-inspired recipes with ingredients from the Pacific Northwest. The linen tablecloths, simple furniture and large windows provide a refined atmosphere which is the perfect accompaniment to the culinary adventure on offer. We particularly enjoyed the lamb shank slow cooked in a beer and cilantro sauce.

NORTHWEST DISTRICT

Area map p. 37

$30–50

14 **St. Jack** – *B4* – *1610 NW 23rd Ave.* – *☎ (503) 360 1281* – *www.stjackpdx. com* – *Mon-Sat 5pm-10pm, Sun 10am-2pm* – *$29/48.* At the heart of trendy, lively NW 23rd Ave. is this French restaurant, which has made a name for itself thanks to a menu that serves classics (snails, foie gras, duck à l'orange) with a twist and based on local fruit and vegetables. There is a well-stocked wine list featuring wines from both Oregon and further afield. The only drawback is that the restaurant is rather noisy.

⑨ Paley's Place Bistro and Bar – *B4* – *1204 NW 21st Ave. – ℘ (503) 243 2403 – www.paleysplace.net – 5pm–9pm (10pm Fri–Sat) – $19/42.* Chef and owner Vitaly Paley works his magic in this Victorian house in Nob Hill. The restaurant, which seats 50, exudes a classical elegance matched in the dishes. Begin your meal with a platter of charcuterie, pâtés and terrines, then move on to sustainably sourced meat, fish and shellfish from around the world. Available in small or large portions.

CENTRAL EASTSIDE

Area maps pp. 16–17 and p. 37

Around $15

㊲ J & M Cafe – *D5* – *537 SE Ash St. – ℘ (503) 284 3366 – jandmcafepdx. com – Mon–Fri 7:30am–2pm, weekend 8am–2pm – $10/15.* With its warm and family-like atmosphere, this no-frills café is a neighborhood institution. Tasty, copious American breakfasts (scrambled eggs, eggs Benedict and filter coffee) are served in the eclectically decorated setting of an old brick warehouse.

④ Kachinka – *D6* – *720 SE Grand Ave. – ℘ (503) 235 0059 – www. kachkapdx.com – 4pm–midnight – $8/14.* You'd be forgiven for thinking you'd stumbled into an Eastern European grandmother's house at this restaurant in the Belmont district,

which channels traditional Russian cuisine through its decor and menu: think beetroot, potatoes, cabbage and hot or cold *zakuski* (appetizers), all served in just the right portion sizes. Vodka fans will be in paradise.

$15–30

㉘ Canard – *D5* – *734 E Burnside St. – ℘ (971) 279 2356 – canardpdx.com – Mon–Fri 8am–midnight, weekend 9am–midnight – $16/20.* Vibrant and noisy, Canard is the neighbor and little brother of famous Le Pigeon (👍 *p. 70*). Here, the atmosphere is more relaxed, the cuisine a touch more accessible and the prices a bit more affordable. The stars of the menu are the tuna tartare, salmon a la plancha and foie gras dumplings. Canard serves excellent cocktails and has a fantastic wine list.

㉚ Olympia Provisions – *D5* – *107 SE Washington St. – ℘ (503) 954 3663 – olympiaprovisions.com – Mon–Fri 11am–10pm, weekend 9am–10pm – Platter of charcuterie $14/34, entrée $15/27.* In a district that has seen industrial buildings converted into smart boutiques and fine-dining restaurants, Olympia Provisions is certainly a major player. Here, charcuterie reigns king with products that rank among the tastiest in the country. There are also well-crafted dishes and a short but well-curated drinks list. We love it!

⑧ Shalom Y'all – *D6* – *117 SE Taylor St. – ℘ (503) 208 3661 – www.shalomyallpdx.com – ♿ – Mon–Fri 11am–10pm, weekend 10am–10pm – Entrée $16/40.* Those with a soft spot for Israeli street food shouldn't miss this place. Shalom Y'all cooks up traditional breads, grilled food and vegetables in the fiery flames of its stone oven, creating exquisite small plates that are perfect for sharing. While the crispy trout and shakshuka are excellent, take a walk on the wild side and go for the kebab with burnt cinnamon, served with freekeh salad, red onions and hummus.

22 Renata – *D6* – *626 SE Main St. – ℘ (503) 954 2708 – www.renatapdx. com – Daily 5pm-9pm – $25.* Exposed beams, walls of windows and warm lighting make this Italian joint ideal for a romantic dinner, but it's also good for kids. The menu is compact; one page of contemporary Italian fare—ricotta gnocchi, beet and blood orange salad, with meat from local farms butchered in house—and a second with Oregon craft beer, and wine of Oregon, neighboring Washington state and Italy. Come warm summer evenings, the patio here is the place to be.

$30–50

20 Le Pigeon – *D5* – *738 E Burnside St. – ℘ (503) 546 8796 – www. lepigeon.com – 5pm-10pm – $24/39.* Gabriel Rucker was one of the first chefs from a Portland restaurant to gain recognition among US food critics, and his success has paved the way for many of his colleagues. In this small dining room with its chic, rustic decor and open kitchen, sample the foie gras profiteroles, lamb, and beef bourguignon, served with local vegetables.

13 Clarklewis Restaurant – *D6* – *1001 SE Water Ave. – ℘ (503) 235 2294 – www.clarklewispdx.com –* ♿

– *11:30am–2pm and 4:30pm–9pm (10pm Fri–Sat), happy hour Mon–Fri 4:30pm–6:30pm – $14/22.* This airy, attractive Italian-inspired restaurant is one of the greats of Portland's food scene. The cuisine is inventive, fresh and full of flavor, and the waiters and bartenders are just as on-trend as the cocktails. Set in a former garage, the restaurant retains an industrial charm, with its large glass doors that open out onto the street. There is a friendly atmosphere, and for those on a shoestring budget it's worth visiting during happy hour.

SOUTHEAST

Area maps pp. 16–17 and p. 37

Around $15

1 Bollywood Theater – *E7* – *3010 SE Division St. – ℘ (503) 477 6699 – www.bollywoodtheaterpdx. com – 11am–10pm – Street food $7/10.50, entrée $10/19.* There's a bohemian, relaxed atmosphere in this airy, pared-back space with its souvenirs from the owners' trips to the Indian subcontinent covering the walls. The dishes, which are flavorful, colorful and served in generous portions, take inspiration from local street food and are a delight to the taste buds at a low price.

32 Scottie's Pizza Parlor – *E7* – *2128 SE Division St. – ℘ (971) 544 7878 – www.scottiespizzaparlor.com – Mon–Sat 11:30am–9pm, Sun noon–8pm, happy hour Mon–Fri 2pm–5pm – Slice of pizza $5, large pizza $20/25.* Crisp, gooey, melt-in-the-mouth and fresh all at once, here they serve some of

Portland's best pizzas, no contest. Square or round, you can't go wrong. From 10pm to midnight the first Friday of every month, the lights go down, the disco ball drops, and from the oven come 28" pies cut into eight giant slices.

$15–30

21 Pok Pok – *F7* – *3226 SE Division St.* – ✆ *(503) 232 1387* – *pokpokdivision.com* – ♿ – *11:30am –10pm* – *$14/21*. This unusually decorated establishment (somewhere between a log cabin and a greasy spoon) is inspired by Thai street food. All of Portland is mad about its warm atmosphere. Given this craze, it's a good idea to book ahead. Is it overrated? Not really, if you take into account the high-quality dishes served, ranging from tender (and sticky) caramelized chicken wings to prawns baked with pork belly. It's a wonderful journey, bursting with colors and spices.

☺ **34 Tasty n Daughters** – *F7* – *4537 SE Division St.* – ✆ *(503) 621 1400* – *www.tastyndaughters.com* – *9am–10pm* – *$14/23*. A favorite of Portlanders, this establishment has a menu that showcases top-notch American cuisine combined with a Mediterranean touch. There's a lively atmosphere and tasty cocktails to boot!

38 Tusk – *E5* – *2448 E Burnside St.* – ✆ *(503) 894 8082* – *www.tuskpdx. com* – *Mon–Thur 5pm–10pm, Fri 5pm– 11pm, Sat 9am–11pm, Sun 9am–10pm* – *$13/34*. The name of this restaurant doesn't instantly shout Middle Eastern food. But here, you'll find it, prepared with local produce and products. The restaurant's famous hummus is complemented with tasty beef or lamb skewers and steamed or grilled vegetables (the seasonal asparagus are fantastic). A symphony of small dishes will fill your table, delighting the senses! The setting is pleasant, the cocktails delicious and, in summer, the terrace is hopping.

☺ **33 Southeast Wine Collective** – *F7* – *2425 SE 35th Place* – ✆ *(503) 208 2061* – *sewinecollective. com* – *Mon 4pm–9pm, Tue–Thur 4pm–10pm, Fri 4pm–11pm, Sat 1pm–11pm, Sun 1pm–9pm* – *$14/23*. At the heart of the vibrant Division district, this winery doubles as a tasting room and restaurant with large windows that open into the wine cellar. Discover excellent wines produced on site and others from small artisan producers around Oregon that are represented by the Southeast Wine Collective. Tuck into well-prepared food created from fresh, local produce. An excellent restaurant.

Over $50

☺ **40 Coquine** – *H6* – *6839 SE Belmont St.* – ✆ *(503) 384 2483* – *coquinepdx.com* – *Brunch: Mon–Thur 9:30am–2:30pm, Fri–Sat 8am–2:30pm; dinner Wed–Sun 5pm–10pm* – *Meal around $30/60*. This restaurant, opened in 2015 by the young French chef Katy Millard, is a top pick in the slightly eccentric district of Mount Tabor in east Portland. It's certainly worth the trip: the restaurant is cozy and elegant with creative dishes on the menu. The pork sugo, sole meunière, and Dungeness crab soup are expertly accompanied with local natural wines. It's customary to leave the restaurant with scandalously gooey chocolate chip cookies to indulge in over breakfast the following day.

NORTH/NORTHEAST

Area map p. 37

Under $15

3 **Bunk** – *E1* – *2017 NE Alberta St. – ℘ (503) 328 2865 – www. bunksandwiches.com – 10am–8pm – $9.50/14.* Perfect for lunch on the go, Bunk's sandwiches are some of the best in town. Particularly recommendable is the roast beef sandwich with caramelized onions, cheddar, and horseradish sauce.

26 **Wolf and Bear's** – *C3* – *3925 N Mississippi Ave. – ℘ (503) 453 5044 – eatwolfandbears.com – 11am–9pm – Pita $9.* In the vibrant Mississippi/Williams district, this food cart, which is actually a charming little vintage caravan-kitchen, serves tasty pitas made from fresh ingredients, taking inspiration from Lebanon and Israel. You'll find plenty of vegetarian and vegan options. There's a large picnic table set up in front of the cart for sunny days.

39 **Koi Fusion** – *C2* – *4237 N Mississippi Ave. – ℘ (971) 888 4127 – koifusionpdx.com – 11:30am–4pm (7pm Fri–Sun) – $8/10.* Also in Mississippi/Williams, another food cart—and favorite with the locals—serves up tasty, invigorating Korean-American fusion cuisine.

15 **¿Por Qué No?** – *C2* – *3524 N Mississippi Ave. – ℘ (503) 467 4149 – www.porquenotacos.com – 11am–10pm (9:30pm Sun) – Tacos $3/5 – Entrée $10/17.* A candy-pink taqueria lit up with lanterns, this restaurant's confined interior is full of decoration that, while slightly kitsch, is genuinely charming. There's also a little terrace, and throughout you'll find a laid-back atmosphere. The margarita could be one of the best in town. They have a second restaurant at 4635 SE Hawthorne Blvd.

$15–30

17 **Toro Bravo** – *D3* – *120 NE Russell St. – ℘ (503) 281 4464 – www. torobravopdx.com – 5pm–8pm (11pm Fri–Sat) – Tapas $7/12 – Entrée $12/24.* Portlanders flock to this popular tapas bar from the moment it opens. The boss's regular trips to Spain with his team are the source of this menu with its wide range of dishes. Don't miss the octopus a la plancha with peppers, the oxtail croquettes with chili mayonnaise, and the sublime Toro Bravo paella made with local shellfish.

18 **Ned Ludd** – *D2* – *3925 NE Martin Luther King Jr Blvd – ℘ (503) 288 6900 – www.nedluddpdx.com – 5pm–10pm – $13/32.* With its rustic decor combining wood and agricultural tools, this restaurant— named after the 18th-century anti-industrial British folk legend—serves dishes cooked in a wood-fired oven, from roasted trout to braised lamb. With its wonderful presentations and frank and candid flavors, this is truly a great restaurant. Monday is pizza night.

© David L. Reamer Photography/Toro Bravo

Toro Bravo

$30–50

㉗ Quaintrelle – *C2* – *3936 N Mississippi Ave.* – ☎ *(503) 200 5787* – *www.quaintrelle.co* – *Wed–Thur and Sun 5pm–9pm, Fri–Sat 5pm–10pm* – *Most sharing plates $14.* The chefs at this bi-level New American restaurant take care with seasonal, local ingredients, turning out plates as pretty as they are delicious. The eggplant with sunchoke, halloumi, labneh and roasted onion petals is a treat. Long wine menu; well-curated cocktail list. Pleasant patio.

⑲ Ox – *D3* – *2225 NE Martin Luther King Jr Blvd* – ☎ *(503) 284 3366* – *oxpdx.com* – *5pm–10pm (11pm Fri–Sat) – Set menu $36/45.* This Argentinian restaurant has seen great success and already has an excellent reputation in Portland. Cooked up on Ox's wood-fired grill are halibut, salmon, octopus, beef and sausages, which are then perfectly accompanied with excellent sauces and generous sides of local veggies (kale, rainbow chard, radishes, etc.). This is a flawless establishment with a well-stocked wine list. Reservations are advised.

㉙ Tournant – *D5* – *920 NE Glisan St.* – ☎ *(503) 206 4463* – *tournantpdx.com* – *See web for schedule.* More than just a restaurant, Tournant is a space for culinary creation based around events *(see website).* No matter what's on, the cuisine is always high-quality, healthy, gourmet and based on a quest for the very best local products. It's ideal for foodies and specializes in oysters.

Over $50

☻ **31** **Beast** – **E1** – *5425 NE 30th Ave. – Reservations: beast@beastpdx.com – www.beastpdx.com – Tue-Sat dinner only, Sun brunch and dinner – Closed Mon – Set menus of 4 dishes $65/90, 6 dishes $118.* One of Portland's most famous (and creative) restaurants features large wooden tables, soft lighting and an open kitchen. The products are extremely well sourced, the presentations bold and daring, and the compositions provide an array of striking flavors. It's an experience that (while pricey) is highly recommended.

OREGON CITY

$15–30

Ingrid's – *209 7th St. – ℘ (503) 744 0457 – ingridsscandinavianfood.com – Wed-Sat noon-8pm, Sun noon-5pm, closed Mon-Tue – Meal around $15/20.* While it seems to be all about Scandinavian specialties, this establishment has a surprise in store, because a good part of the menu is dedicated to...Korean classics! Korean BBQ or Norwegian meatballs...it's up to you.

AROUND MOUNT HOOD

$15–30

Ant Farm Cafe and Bakery – *39140 Proctor Blvd – Sandy – ℘ (503) 668 9955 – www.antfarmyouthservices.com – 7am-3pm – Meal around $15/20.* While not exactly revolutionary, the menu is pleasant, with its generous

salads and tasty sandwiches made with carefully selected products. The setting is lovely and spacious, with cozy areas and works of art on the walls.

Koya Kitchen – *67886 US 26 – Welches – ℘ (503) 564 9345 – koya. kitchen – Noon-9pm – Meal around $15/20.* Somewhere between a food cart and roadside café, Koya serves up an authentic Japanese smattering of noodles, salads and sautéed vegetables in a wooded setting. There is a wide sake and craft beer selection and a charming outside area with large wooden tables, lanterns and hammocks.

TUALATIN VALLEY

Around $15

Ridgewalker Brewing Company – *1921 21st Ave. - Forest Grove – ℘ (503) 747 0271 – www.ridgewalkerbrewing.com – 11am-10pm – Salad $9/12, sandwich $10/14.* A huge fan of beer, this microbrewery's young owner started making a name for himself in his parents' garage. The small business has since grown and the establishment now has thirty different types of beer on tap, as well as American fare (tacos, burgers, salads, etc.).

WILLAMETTE VALLEY

Around $15

Red Hills Market – *155 SW 7th St. - Dundee – ℘ (971) 832 8414 – www. redhillsmarket.com – 7am-8pm – $9/14.* This is a market with warm decor where you can stock up on great-quality products or recharge your batteries in the restaurant. There are pizzas baked in a wood oven, generous sandwiches, and gourmet soups—something for everybody. It's a great place to visit. Just opposite is Dundee Bistro, a more chic locale with an intimate atmosphere, and excellent cooking too.

Around $100

The Painted Lady – *201 S College St. – Newberg – ☎ (503) 538 3850 – thepaintedladyrestaurant.com – 5pm–10pm – Closed Mon–Tue – Set menu $95/110.* This restaurant set in a Victorian house is renowned for the sophisticated presentation of its dishes. The ingredients all come from the nearby ocean or local farms and the menus are changed on a regular basis.

MCMINNVILLE

$15–30

Nick's Italian Café – *521 NE 3rd St. – ☎ (503) 434 4471 – nicksitaliancafe.com – ♿ – 5pm–9pm – Pizza $15/17 – Entrée $16/29.* A safe bet in McMinnville. The gourmet, generously portioned pizzas will not disappoint and the dishes are extremely well prepared from local products (mushrooms from the nearby woods, lamb from local farms, shellfish from the nearby coast, etc.). There is also an excellent wine list featuring wines from the valley. Service with a smile.

$30–50

The Barberry – *645 NE 3rd St. – ☎ (503) 857 0457 – www.thebarberry.com – Weekend brunch 9am–3pm – $26/40.* On the main thoroughfare of this wine-producing city, this restaurant is an excellent option in the Willamette Valley. Ninety-five percent of the products are from Oregon, the wine list is very impressive, the bar has a remarkable whiskey and cocktail menu and, to top it off, there's a pleasant rooftop terrace.

OREGON COAST

$15–30

Baked Alaska – *1 12th St. – Pier 12, on the Riverwalk – Astoria – ☎ (503) 325-7414 – www.bakedak.com – 11:30am–9pm (10pm Fri–Sat) – Entrée $15/28, menu $39.* From the dining room of this restaurant on stilts, you get superb views over the Columbia River mouth. The chef concocts tasty Northwestern fare from fresh, high-quality fish and shellfish. The salmon with crisp vegetables melts in the mouth. The menu also includes pizzas, salads and sandwiches, as well as small platters of cheese and charcuterie, goose confit and mushroom ragout.

Where to drink

In Portland the drinks are artisan, local, organic and alternative. Throughout the city, the dishwater coffee of the diners of old has been replaced with delicious third wave java, roasted on site. With 75 microbreweries listed in 2019, Portland certainly lives up to its nickname "Beervana." Natural wines have recently taken the trendy and intimate modern bars by storm, from **the Pearl District** to the **Eastside**. But the true Portland tradition is still the dive bar, a casual neighborhood spot where you can tuck in to tacos or fries and wash them down with a draft beer. Stay until the early hours, surrounded by a slightly weird bunch of locals. These gems are mostly found in the Alberta Arts District and Laurelhurst, which are in **Northeast**. Trendy and modern **Downtown** and **the Pearl District** also have plenty of rooftop bars and elegant cocktail spots.

♿ Find the addresses on our maps using the number in the listing (for example ❶). The coordinates in red (for example C2) refer to the detachable map (inside the cover).

DOWNTOWN

Area map pp. 16–17

Bars

❶ Multnomah Whiskey Library – *C5* – 1124 SW Alder St. – ✆ (503) 954 1381 – mwlpdx.com – 4pm–11:15pm (0:15am Fri–Sat) – Closed Sun. This is a Portland highlight with its spectacular wall of softly lit bottles behind an old wooden bar, Chesterfield easy chairs, brick walls and tapestries. The service is extremely professional and while the menu is limited, the high quality of the food perfectly matches the elegant surroundings. A chic and refined establishment where you can feel completely at ease.

❷ Jackknife – *C5* – 614 SW 11th Ave. – ✆ (503) 384 2347 – jackknifepdx.com – Mon–Wed 3pm–1am, Thur–Sat 3pm–2am, Sun 3pm–midnight. The bar at the Sentinel hotel (*♿ Where to stay*) is vast, lively and loud, perfect to round off the night. Its drinks menu is eclectic, with something for everybody. Under soft lighting, the background tracks feature rock classics and 80s hits.

❸ Pépé le Moko – *C5* – 407 SW 10th Ave. – ✆ (503) 546 8537 – pepelemokopdx.com – 4pm–2am. This speakeasy bears the name of an old gangster film starring Jean Gabin (1937). It has an intimate atmosphere with jazz background music and quiet nooks popular with couples. They serve excellent cocktails, and there's a limited menu for anyone who fancies a little sandwich.

❹ Oregon Wines On Broadway– *C5* – 515 SW Broadway – ✆ (503) 228 4655 – www.oregonwinesonbroadway. com – Noon–8pm – Closed Sun. While the understated facade doesn't look particularly promising, this small, narrow bar certainly knows how to look after fans of Oregon's pinot noir. There is an abundant selection

77

of excellent wines, offered by glass, bottle or as flights (for a wine tasting).

Cafés

5 Courier Coffee Roasters – *C5* – *923 SW Oak St.* – ☎ *(503) 545 6444* – *www.couriercoffeeroasters.com* – ♿ – *Mon–Fri 7am–6pm, weekend 9am–5pm – Closed Jan 1 and Dec 25.* A small establishment where you can drink excellent coffee and feast upon homemade pastries. The owners didn't use to have a brick and mortar space, and delivered their coffee by bike. Thanks to their success, you can now sample their coffee in this café with its pared-back decor.

6 Stumptown Coffee Roasters – *C5* – *128 SW 3rd Ave.* – ☎ *(855) 711 3385* – *www.stumptowncoffee.com* – *Mon–Fri 6am–7pm, weekend 7am–7pm.* Portland's first artisan coffee roaster is something of an institution. Regulars, who sip fair trade coffee while tapping away at their laptops, can't stop coming back for more. And as you might expect in Portland, there's a cool, laid-back ambiance. They have four other cafés around town.

© L. Decoudin/Michelin

Tope

OLD TOWN/CHINATOWN

Area map pp. 16–17

Bars

7 Tope – *C5* – *15 NW 4th Ave.* – ☎ *(503) 770 0500* – *thehoxton.com* – *Tue–Thur 4pm–11pm, Fri–Sat 4pm–midnight, Sun–Mon 4pm–10pm.* The white tiled walls, green plants and wooden tables create a pleasant setting in this bar/taqueria on the top floor of the Hoxton hotel (♿ *Where to stay*). If you add the rather spectacular view over Portland's rooftops and the excellent cocktails (try the mezcal), there are ample reasons to drop by.

8 Basement – *C5* – *15 NW 4th Ave.* – ☎ *(503) 770 0500* – *thehoxton.com* – *5pm–midnight – Closed Mon–Tue.* This charming speakeasy bar in the Hoxton hotel basement (♿ *Where to stay*) ticks all the boxes of the genre, with its dark, discreet atmosphere, low lighting and lit-up wall of bottles behind the bar. They serve excellent cocktails and a small menu of tasty American-Chinese food.

PEARL DISTRICT

Area map pp. 16–17

Bars

9 Teardrop – *C5* – *1015 NW Everett St.* – ☎ *(503) 445 8109* – *www.teardroplounge.com* – *From 4pm.* Another cocktail bar with a more cool and trendy feel. The space is understated, with bare walls and a large circular bar where you can sit and watch the excellent cocktails being created. Great people watching, too.

Warmed Brownie, Hazelnuts & Hot Fudge Sundae, Salt and Straw

80

😊 **11 Thelonious Wines** – *C5* – 516 NW 9ᵗʰ Ave. – ☎ (503) 444 7447 – theloniouswines.com – Mon-Fri 4pm-9pm, Sat noon-9pm, Sun noon-7pm. On the first floor, a wonderfully stocked wine cellar with gems from Burgundy and Bordeaux welcomes you for tasting sessions (*for a fee*). Upstairs on the cozy mezzanine are voluptuous club chairs where you can savor your glass of wine to the melodies from the turntable.

NORTHWEST

Area map p. 37

Bars

10 The Old Portland Wine Bar – *B4* – 1433 NW Quimby St. – ☎ (503) 621 7103 – theoldportland.com – Wed-Sat 5pm-10pm. Courtney Taylor, the singer of the highly regarded rock band The Dandy Warhols, opened this bar in 2017. Passionate about aged Bordeaux wines, he has conjured up a place with a rock-and-roll spirit (posters covering the walls, reclaimed materials and background music to fit) and some lovely vintages on offer. This is the epitome of cool.

Ice cream shops

12 Salt and Straw – *B4* – *838 NW 23rd Ave.* – *(971) 271 8168* – *saltandstraw.com* – *10am–11pm.* The most famous ice cream shop in Portland fits perfectly into the city's philosophy: here you'll find local and organic products that support the local economy. All of the ice creams are absolutely impeccable taste-wise, but the daring flavors are the stars of the show: besides the usual classics, you can also find sweet potato, goat cheese and even beer ice cream!

CENTRAL EASTSIDE

Area maps *pp. 16–17 and p. 37*

Bars

13 Elvis Room – *D5* – *203 SE Grand Ave.* – *(503) 235 5690* – *4pm–2:30am.* On the first floor is a 1960s starlet's boudoir, complete with a very ornate and glamorous counter. In the basement is a mysterious hideaway with stained-glass windows. There are cocktails everywhere, typical Portland bar food, and walls decorated with daubs of laughing sixties nudes and bright-eyed languishing angora cats. It's a real institution.

14 Rontoms – *D5* – *600 E Burnside St.* – *(503) 236 4536* – *www.rontoms.net* – *Mon–Fri 11am–2:30pm, weekend 2pm–2:30am.* Opening out on to the street, this beautiful, spacious bar has a huge terrace that is hidden away from the world. There's a trendy ambiance, and indie rock and folk bands play most evenings.

22 Hey Love – *D5* – *920 E Burnside St.* – *(503) 206-6223* – *heylovepdx.com* – *Daily until 2am.* It's Club Tropicana all year round at this Portland bar. Hey Love is one of bars of the Jupiter Next Hotel (*Where to stay*) and it certainly channels summer vibes. The waiters wear Hawaiian shirts, lush plants line the walls, and the warm colors and cocktails at sunset all help to conjure up the ambiance of Honolulu. There's a lively, party atmosphere in the evening.

15 The Lovecraft – *D5* – *421 SE Grand Ave.* – *thelovecraftbar.com* – *Sun–Thur 8pm–2:15am, Fri–Sat 4pm–2:15am.* While the gothic and somewhat kitschy decoration may put some people off, industrial, dark wave and minimal wave music fans will find just what they're looking for. The bar's low prices also attract broke students. There's a small dance floor to let your hair down to the sound of hits by The Cure and local bands.

Microbreweries

29 Hair of the Dog – *D6* – *61 SE Yamhill St.* – *(503) 232 6585* – *www.hairofthedog.com* – *11:30am–10pm, (8pm Sun) – Closed Mon.* This is a huge space with high ceilings and heavy wooden beams. There's an interesting selection of home-brewed beers and some specialties that are worth a try, including peach beer, cherry beer and an imperial stout aged 15 months in bourbon barrels. Make the most of the terrace on sunny days.

30 Base Camp Brewing Company – *D5* – *930 SE Oak St.* – *(503) 477 7479* – *basecampbrewingco.com* – *Sun–Thur Noon–10pm, Fri–Sat 11am–midnight.* The imposing tasting room perfectly captures the spirit of this establishment, decorated with photos of climbing, rafting and other outdoor sports. There are plenty of beers with character, including our favorite, the Nomadic Double IPA.

SOUTHEAST

Area map *p. 37*

Bars

16 **The Liquor Store** – *F6* – *3341 SE Belmont St. –* 🎧 *(503) 754-7782 – www.theliquorstorepdx.com – 4pm-2:30am.* The ultimate rock bar, as dark and mysterious as a Jim Jarmusch film, the Liquor Store has cult records lining the walls (ask the bartender if you want to take a closer look). An old photo booth invites you to take your picture with a melancholic expression and a Patti Smith track playing in the background; downstairs, musicians perform on a very dark, very cool indie stage. Try the superb cocktails.

17 **Enoteca Nostrana** – *D6* – *1401 SE Morrison St. –* 🎧 *(503) 234 2427 – www.enotecanostrana.com – 4pm-midnight.* Here there's a formidable wine list with natural wines from all over the world and refined cocktails, made by an all-female staff. There's a huge amount of choice in this 80s-decor bar inspired by the daring designs and architecture of the Memphis Group. Pastel and turquoise colors, soft lighting and modern furniture decorate this original and chic but unpretentious bar.

18 **Bar Norman** – *E7* – *12615 SE Clinton St. –* *barnorman.com – 4pm-11pm (midnight Fri-Sat) – Closed Sun.* Opened in summer 2018 by the sommelier Dana Frank, this bar is an

ode to the wine bars of the Old World. Here you can raise a glass of natural, organic, reasonably priced wine, to the sound of contemporary beats. The understated, trendy setting doesn't prevent the clientele of mostly forty- and fifty-somethings from getting tipsy in style.

Cafés

19 **Pied Cow** – *F6* – *3244 SE Belmont St. –* 🎧 *(503) 230-4866 – Mon-Thur 4pm-midnight, Fri 4pm-1am, Sat noon-1am, Sun noon-midnight.* This cult café in a lovely, slightly crooked Victorian house is eclectically decorated with antique furnishings and some sagging velvet sofas. Settle in for a cinnamon tea and glass of red with friends or treat yourself to a slice of cake while savoring a cool, psychedelic play list, far from the urban bustle.

20 **Dots Cafe** – *E7* – *2521 SE Clinton St. –* 🎧 *(503) 235 0203 – dotscafeportland.com – Mon-Sat noon-2:30am, Sun 10am-2:30am.* By day, a rock'n'roll diner welcomes locals from the bohemian Clinton/Division district for a cup of coffee. By night, beers, burgers and cheap cocktails await partygoers in a relaxed atmosphere.

NORTH/NORTHEAST

Area maps *pp. 16–17 and p. 37*

Bars

21 **Laurelthirst Public House** – *E5* – *2958 NE Glisan St. –* 🎧 *(503) 232 1504 – www.laurelthirst.com – Mon-Tue 4pm-midnight, Wed-Thur 4pm-1am, Fri 4pm-2am, Sat 11am-2am, Sun 11am-midnight.* This authentic rock and country bar—with great prices—welcomes local bands to its small stage with a familial, bohemian atmosphere. Dance the night away in cowboy boots and meet old Willamette seamen out smoking on the sidewalk. Here, young people mix with the regulars and everything is just as it was before gentrification.

㉓ Sardine Head – *C1* – *5202 N Albina Ave.* – ☏ *(503) 209 2091* – *pennsardinpdx.com* – *6pm–11pm (midnight Fri–Sat)*. This bar has one of the best natural wine lists in Portland and some inventive light bites. The trendy clientèle are welcomed into a refined space done up in light wood tones, with a handful of tables and a bar kept by friendly sommeliers.

㉔ The Alibi Tiki Lounge – *C2* – *4024 N Interstate Ave.* – ☏ *(503) 287 5335* – *www.alibiportland.com* – *11:30am–2:30am*. Since 1947, the best tiki bar in town, in all its kitschness, has evoked the warm nights of Polynesia. Shell lamps, languid lei-wearing mermaids, the typical exotic cocktails, rattan and palm trees: this is the 1950s America South Pacific dream in all its glory. Add a little uninhibited karaoke where friends can let their hair down and you're guaranteed the night of your life.

㉕ Alleyway – *E1* – *2415 NE Alberta St.* – ☏ *(503) 287 7760* – *3pm–2:30am*. At the heart of the Alberta Arts District, a clientèle of tattoo-covered, indie-rock customers fit right in at this clapped-out dive bar with its pool table, pinball machines, vending machine selling sex toys and levels of alcohol that mean it's definitely a good idea to call a cab for the return journey.

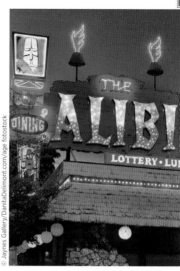

© Jaynes Gallery/DanitaDelimont.com/age fotostock

Alibi Tiki Lounge

㉖ Bye and Bye – *D1* – *1011 NE Alberta St.* – ☏ *(503) 281 0537* – *thebyeandbye. com* – *Noon–2am*. Still in Alberta, this cool, unpretentious bar has reasonably priced cocktails, local beers on tap and great vegan snacks.

㉗ Prost! – *C2* – *4237 N Mississippi Ave.* – ☏ *(503) 954 2674* – *prostportland.com* – *Mon–Fri 11:30am –2:30am, weekend 11am–2:30am*. This traditional German pub, with its sunny beer garden, is found in the vibrant Mississippi/Williams district. You'll find German and Belgian beers as well as Bavarian sausages and pretzels.

㉘ Expatriate – *E1*– *5424 NE 30th Ave.* – ☏ *(503) 867 5309* – *expatriatepdx.com* – *5pm–midnight*. There's a retro chic ambiance with East and Southeast Asian overtones in this bar. Popular with purists, it features a short menu of beautifully crafted cocktails (our favorite: Dead Romans). There's great food (the Laotian tacos) and, as is often the case in Portland, excellent indie rock background music.

Cafés

31 Cup & Bar – *D5* – *118 NE Martin Luther King Jr Blvd* – *☏ (503) 388 7701* – *www.cupandbar.com* – *7am–7pm.* In a district that has been revitalized by a host of real estate projects and new businesses, Cup & Bar is one of our favorites. It's the perfect place to ready yourself for a day of sightseeing, with succulent chocolate pastries (made on site) and a tea or artisan coffee. Tours of the chocolate production area and coffee roastery are available on request.

32 Barista – *E1* – *1725 NE Alberta St.* – *baristapdx.com* – *Mon–Fri 6am–6pm, weekend 7am–6pm.* This beautiful, airy café, which combines Parisian chairs with rustic dark wood decor, serves nothing but cups of absolute perfection.

33 Either/Or – *D2* – *4003 N Williams Ave.* – *☏ (503) 208 3475* – *eitherorpdx. com* – *7am–10pm (midnight Thur–Sat).* By day, excellent third wave coffee, breakfasts and brunches; by night cocktails and DJs. The versatility of this chic 70s establishment brings the Mississippi/Williams creative district to life.

34 Proud Mary – *E1* – *2012 NE Alberta St.* – *☏ (503) 208 3475* – *proudmarycoffee.com* – *Mon–Fri 7am–4pm, weekend 8am–4pm.* Set off on a round-the-world tour of coffee in

this establishment run by an Australian team. They serve high-end coffee and aim to reduce the distance between producers and consumers. It's a vast, airy setting with a relaxed atmosphere (it almost goes without saying in Portland). There's excellent food: try the best-selling potato hash with home-smoked bacon, kale salad and a poached egg.

OREGON CITY

Oregon City Brewing Company – *1401 Washington St.* – *☏ (503) 908 1948* – *www.ocbeerco.com* – *11am–11pm (10pm Sun).* Just like everywhere else in Oregon, the small town of Oregon City is well stocked with microbreweries (there are three in town, as well as a cider works). Oregon City Brewing Company has a tasting room with 40 beers on tap. Don't miss their The Bryce is Right, a slightly lemony IPA with just the right degree of bitterness.

AROUND MOUNT HOOD

Clackamas River Growlers – *367 SE Main St.* – *Estacada* – *☏ (503) 630 2739* – *clackamasrivergrowlers.com* – *Mon 5pm–9pm, Tue–Thur 3pm–9pm, Fri 2pm–9pm, Sat noon–9pm, Sun 2pm–7pm.* This is the beating heart of the small town of Estacada. There's a warm ambiance and the beer and ciders come in abundance (there are 32 on tap). There's a tiny menu of standard but tasty bar grub (think pizza, sausage, Bavarian pretzels), or you can bring in takeaway from nearby restaurants.

Shopping

Whether you're looking for vintage clothing, passionate designers, arts and crafts shops, eccentric flea markets, specialist bookstores, tiny record stores or distilleries (and we mustn't forget the unbeatable local doughnuts), you'll find what you're looking for in Portland. From **Old Town** to the **Eastside**, a wealth of independent boutiques provide a host of alternatives to the mass consumerism that reigns elsewhere in the US. And the fact that there's *no sales tax* means that you can treat yourself without breaking the bank. The big chains and brands are found in **Northwest** and **Downtown**, around **Pioneer District Court**.

♿ Find the addresses on our maps using the number in the listing (for example ①). The coordinates in red (for example C2) refer to the detachable map (inside the cover).

DOWNTOWN

Area map pp. 16–17

Fashion and decor

① **Union Way** – *C5* – *1022 W Burnside St.* – *☏ (503) 235 5743* – *11am–7pm.* This small, elegant shopping arcade at the heart of Downtown is home to stylish boutiques like Danner, which sells Northwest-style clothing along with their famous boots.

② **Canoe** – *C6* – *1233 SW 10th Ave.* – *☏ (503) 889 8545* – *canoe.design* – *Tue–Sat 10am–6pm, Sun 11am–5pm – Closed Mon.* This boutique selling furnishings and interiors accessories has lovely items that are both practical and well-designed.

Fashion

㉓ **Wildfang** – *D6* – *404 SW 10th Ave* – *☏ (503) 964 6746* – *www.wildfang.com* – *Sun–Thurs 11am–8pm, Fri–Sat 10am–8pm.* Selling super trendy, feminist clothing and plundering the masculine wardrobe to create modern lines, this store reflects Portland's bohemian and activist spirit. A percentage of profits goes to The Trevor Project, an organization providing suicide prevention services to LGBTQ young people.

Records

③ **Tender Loving Empire** – *C5* – *412 SW 10th Ave.* – *☏ (503) 243 5859* – *tenderlovingempire.com* – *10:30am–6:30pm.* Created by the founder of a famous Portland independent label, this boutique cleverly offers records by local bands signed to the label alongside local handicrafts.

Bakeries

④ **Blue Star Donuts** – *C5* – *1155 SW Morrison St., #102* – *☏ (503) 265 8410* – *bluestardonuts.com* – *7am–7pm.* This chain, which has several stores in town, makes its doughnuts from a French brioche recipe and is considered by many to be a leader in its field. They use organic ingredients and quality certainly prevails over quantity.

Farmers' markets

*The main ones are found in the **Cultural District** (at Shemanski Park, between SW Park Ave. and SW Salmon St. – May 1–Oct 30: Wed 10am–2pm), and at **Portland State University** (SW Park Ave. and SW Montgomery St. – Mar–Oct: Sat 8:30am–2pm; Nov–Feb: Sat 9am–2pm). Here, hundreds of stalls sell fresh products from the Greater Portland area (♿ p. 136).*

Confectionery and gadgets

❺ Moonstruck – *C5* – *608 SW Alder St. – ℘ (503) 241 0955 – moonstruckchocolate.com – Mon–Fri 8am–8pm, Sat 10am–8pm, Sun 10am–6pm.* Truffles, caramels, bars, bark, and hot cocoa mix are sold at this tiny shop. The PDX Carpet dark chocolate bar ($12) makes a great souvenir-gift. *(Pearl District branch at 526 NW 23rd Ave.)*

OLD TOWN/CHINATOWN

Area map *pp. 16–17*

Arts and crafts

❽ Portland Saturday Market – *C5* – *2 SW Naito Parkway – ℘ (503) 222 6072 – www.portlandsaturdaymarket. com – March to Christmas Eve: Sat 10am–5pm, Sun 11am–4:30pm.* Bohemian, eco-friendly and imaginative, the biggest open-air arts and crafts market in the US is emblematic of Portland's cheerful, community-based free spirit. Created in 1974, it houses 252 arts and crafts stalls from across the Pacific

Northwest. It comes as no surprise that these stalls—selling cushions, medicinal herb mixes, T-shirts with messages, carved wooden items and jewelry—rub shoulders with food carts serving cuisine from around the world for just a few dollars.

Antiques

❻ Hoodoo Antiques – *C5* – *122 NW Couch St. – ℘ (503) 360-3409 – www. hoodooantiques.com – Thur–Sun 11am–4:30pm (noon Sun).* A visit to this antiques shop is both a trip down memory lane and a journey into the unbridled imagination of its friendly owner. Giant plastic sharks, papier-mâché animals, 1950s Christmas decorations and neon signs create a completely nutty universe that is simultaneously full of charm.

Bakeries

❾ Voodoo Doughnut – *C5* – *22 SW 3rd Ave. – ℘ (503) 241 4704 – www. voodoodoughnut.com – ✉ – Open 24/7 – Closed Jan 1st, Thanksgiving and Dec 25th.* A legendary place! You can tell you're getting close when you start to see passers-by with small pink cardboard boxes. Enter this psychedelic world and discover piles of increasingly extravagant doughnuts in a riot of flavors and colors. Don't be put off by the long line; you have to go at least once.

Books

❿ Floating World Comics – *C5* – *400 NW Couch St. – ℘ (503) 241 0227 – www.floatingworldcomics.com – 11am–7pm.* This lovely independent bookstore, dedicated to comics from around the world, is a treasure trove of

manga, graphic novels and other rare or sought-after fanzines.

Fashion

⑪ Unspoken – *C5* – *219 NW Couch St.* – ☎ *(503) 208 3660* – *www.unspokenpdx.com* – *Noon-7pm (5pm Sun)* – *Closed Mon.* A small store selling streetwear for trendy men. Pick up items from brands like Pleasure, Carhartt and Nike, as well as from local designers.

⑫ MadeHere PDX – *C5* – *40 NW 10th Ave.* – ☎ *(503) 224-0122* – *www.madehereonline.com* – *Sun-Fri 11am-6pm, Thur 11am-7pm, Sat 10am-7pm.* Portland designers can show off and sell their wares here, be they jewelery, leather goods, clothes or home decor. This is an elegant space for quality products that do, admittedly, cost a pretty penny.

⑫ Orox Leather Goods – *C5* – *450 NW Couch St.* – ☎ *(503) 954 2593* – *www.oroxleather.com* – *Mon-Sat 10am-5pm.* Orox spans four generations of leather makers. With its roots in Oaxaca, Mexico, it is a reservoir of craft knowledge, creating high-quality products for a range of budgets. You'll be given a warm welcome.

Teas

⑭ Qi Fine Teas – *C5* – *512 NW 9th Ave.* – ☎ *(503) 3477 4853* – *qifineteas.com* – *Noon-9pm.* This is probably the most refined tea house in town and the place to taste, and take home, nearly 60 varieties of tea. Take a seat around a communal table shared with other customers—like in an authentic Chinese tea house—as an

exquisite brew is served, at no cost, by Ivy Zu, a true tea connoisseur. The traditional tea cups and pots, all from the Jingdezhen region in China, are breathtakingly delicate.

PEARL DISTRICT

Area map *pp. 16–17*

Books

⑦ Powell's City of Books – *C5* – *1005 W Burnside St.* – ☎ *(800) 878 7323* – *www.powells.com* – *9am-11pm. Free guided tour on Sundays at 10am (lasting 45min).* This "city of books" is the largest bookstore in the world. It takes up an entire block and contains over a million books. This local institution was in fact born in Chicago in 1970 when the student Michael Powell decided to open an independent bookstore. Inspired by his success, his father, Walter Powell, opened his own bookstore, this time in Portland. In 1979, father and son joined forces to open Powell's, a unique bookstore at the time, with new and second-hand books found side-by-side on the shelves. Today, it's Emily Powell, Michael's daughter, who runs this company with its progressive, humane values.

NORTHWEST

Area map *p. 37*

Distilleries

⑮ Freeland Spirits – *A4* – *2671 NW Vaughn St.* – ☎ *(971) 279 5692* – *freelandspirits.com* – *Wed-Sun from 3pm, distillery tours by request.*

Specializing in gins, bourbons and whiskeys, Freeland is one of the rare distilleries run entirely by women (barely 1% globally). Every last detail is carefully chosen, from the elegant bottle design to the selection of grains (bought from Oregon farmers) and aging methods in oak casks (with a final rest in pinot noir casks for the bourbon).

Fine foods

16 **The Meadow** – *B4* – 805 NW 23rd Ave. – ℘ (503) 305 3388 – themeadow.com – 10am–7pm. Mark Bitterman is familiar with all the facets of salt and chocolate. Hop on board a fascinating gourmet trip around the world through his products. Browse the wine and condiments also sold here. There is a second store at 3731 N Mississippi Ave.

CENTRAL EASTSIDE

Area maps pp. 16–17 and p. 37

Distilleries

17 **Westward Whiskey** – *D5* – 65 SE Washington St. – ℘ (503) 235 3174 – www.westwardwhiskey.com – Noon–7pm (8pm Fri–Sat) – Tours of the distillery every hour. Westward is one of the leaders of the resurgence of craft distilleries in the US and the producer of Westward Whiskey, an American single malt. Discover a number of great spirits such as Krogstad Aquavit, Volstead Vodka and a limited edition line.

18 **New Deal Distillery** – *D6* – 900 SE Salmon St. – ℘ (503) 234 2513 – newdealdistillery.com – Wed–Sun noon–6pm. This distillery, which is

far smaller than Westward, produces around fifteen different alcoholic beverages, including a fresh and expressive Pear Brandy (pears are widely grown in Oregon) and an astonishing Cascadia liquor (with herbs creating a flavor that is somewhere between gin and chartreuse). Sip an excellent cocktail in the tasting room.

Games

19 **Guardian Games** – *D6* – 345 SE Taylor St. – ℘ (503) 238 4000 – ggportland.com – 10am–10pm (8pm Sun). Fans of card games, board games and role-playing games can come and add to their collections at this huge, well-stocked warehouse.

Photo by NashCO/Travel Portland

New Deal Distillery

Home decor and gifts

⓴ Cargo – *D6* – *81 SE Yamhill St. – ℰ (503) 209 8349 – cargoinc.com – 11am–6pm.* Ghanaian rugs, Thai carnival headdresses, Chinese lanterns and bowls, Mexican dolls, Indian movie posters... Like a huge container opening out onto the street, this warehouse-store provides a wonderful sample of crafts from around the world.

Teas

㉑ Smith Teamaker – *D5* – *110 SE Washington St. – ℰ (503) 719 8752 – smithtea.com – 10am–6pm.* In an attractively fitted-out warehouse, you can watch tea being produced through a glass window. There are a few tables where you can sit and taste the fine blends (almost all organic) made in this Portland institution. Pick up a present, like a sachet of Rose City Genmaïcha, a blend of green Japanese tea with roasted rice, rose petals and honey.

Fine foods

㉒ Jacobsen Salt Co. – *D6* – *602 SE Salmon St. – ℰ (503) 719 4973 – jacobsensalt.com – Mon–Sat 10am–5pm, Sun 11am–5pm.* Specializing in salt, Jacobsen Salt Co. sells the precious Pacific Northwest crystals in all shapes and sizes, presented in delightful packages. Salted caramels and chocolates are also given pride of place and make superb gifts.

SOUTHEAST

Area map p. 37

Fashion

㉔ Xtabay Vintage – *E7* – *2515 SE Clinton St. – ℰ (503) 230 2899 – xtabayvintage.com – Thur–Sun 11am–6pm.* Like a boudoir for the glamorous women of days gone by, this vintage fashion boutique has an extremely refined selection of clothes with carefully studied details. High-quality luxury pieces, designer items and fashion brands of a bygone era (Pucci, Schiaparelli, Dior) vie for your attention on the elegant racks.

Bakeries

㉕ Saint Cupcake – *F6* – *3300 SE Belmont St. – ℰ (503) 235 0078 – saintcupcake.com – 11am–7pm (5pm Sun).* While the traditional Portland sweet treats are definitely doughnuts, this lovely bakery seems to have found a recipe for success with its adorable artisan cupcakes in tangy pop colors. There are four branches across town. The cookies, ice cream and tarts are also very tasty.

Records

☺ ㉖ Clinton Street Record & Stereo – *E7* – *2510 SE Clinton St. – ℰ (503) 235 5323 – clintonstreetrecordandstereo.com – 1:30pm–7pm.* A veritable gold mine for music fans, from house to dark wave, boogie to Italo disco, this record store selects its albums with passion. You can also snap up a vintage turntable.

NORTH/NORTHEAST

Shopping malls

27 **Lloyd Center** – *D4* – *2201 Lloyd Center (at the intersection of NE 9th Ave. and Multnomah)* – ℘ *(503) 282 2511* – *www.lloydcenter.com* – ♿ – *Mon–Sat 10am–9pm, Sun 11am–6pm – Opening hours vary by store.* The biggest shopping mall in Oregon, with almost 200 stores, the Lloyd Center also houses restaurants, a movie theater, and an indoor skating rink.

Bakeries

28 **Pip's Original Doughnuts** – *G2* – *4759 NE Fremont St.* – ℘ *(503) 206 8692* – *www.pipsoriginal.com* – *8am–4pm.* Pip's is a rising star on the local doughnut scene. The small doughnuts are fried to order and served hot. Try the surprising bacon and maple syrup doughnut. They also serve wonderful chai.

Home decor and gifts

29 **Paxton Gate** – *C2* – *4204 N Mississippi Ave.* – ℘ *(503) 719 4508* – *paxtongate.com* – *11am–7pm.* This fascinating curiosity shop—with its stuffed animals, crystals, unique home decor, strange plants, books of witchcraft and wizardry and manuals for chemistry enthusiasts—will delight all romantic and gothic souls as well as fans of Portland's specialty: weirdness.

30 **Workshop Vintage** – *D2* – *4011 N Williams Ave.* – ℘ *(503) 206 5813* – *workshopvintage.com* – *11am–7pm (6pm Sun).* This vast boutique sells vintage home decor (1950s metal record stands and magazine racks, tiki cocktail sets, etc.) and creations by local artisans that make lovely presents to take back with you (perfumes, jewelry, hats, etc.) as well as a selection of very retro and trendy second-hand clothing.

31 **Sunlan Lighting Inc** – *C2* – *3901 N Mississippi Ave.* – ℘ *(503) 281 0453* – *sunlanlighting.com* – *Mon–Fri 8am–5:30pm, Sat 10am–5:30pm – Closed Sun.* This is a real Mississippi/Williams institution. Dedicated to light bulbs of all shapes and colors and to some very imaginative home decor, it is managed by a cartoon fan who won't let you leave without one of her drawings. Warning: voltage can vary from country to country, so ask the owner for her advice before setting your heart on a light bulb with a message or light-up Father Christmas.

32 **Cord** – *E1* – *2916 NE Alberta St.* – ℘ *(971) 717 6925* – *cordpdx.com* – *11am–6pm (5pm Sun) – Closed Mon.* There's everything you could ever need for camping and life in the great outdoors—or in your Portland yard—and much of it is handmade in Oregon. That's the principle behind this great little boutique selling exceptionally elegant items: pocketknives, flasks, solar lamps and campfire frying pans.

For your pets

33 **Salty's** – *C2* – *4039 N Mississippi Ave.* – ℘ *(503) 249 1432* – *saltyspetsupply.com* – *11am–8pm (7pm weekends).* There's zero waste at this pet shop, which sells locally-produced organic dry food in bulk for cats and dogs, plus hundreds of types of wet food and essential oils to treat viruses, bacteria and other pet problems.

Nightlife

With its huge variety, Portland's **music scene** is the star of the night, hands down. Listen to small local bands in bars across the **Eastside** (👤 *Where to drink*), opera in **Downtown**, and the biggest names in indie rock playing legendary concert halls from **Old Town** to the North/Northeast Side, and especially in the **Mississippi/Williams** district. Portland isn't particularly a hot spot for clubbing, and the clubs are few and far between. However, it is well-known that Portlanders are young at heart and can spend whole evenings playing arcade games.

👤 *Find the addresses on our maps using the number in the listing (for example ①). The coordinates in red (for example C2) refer to the detachable map (inside the cover).*

92

CLASSICAL MUSIC, OPERA, AND THEATER

① **Portland'5 Centers for the Arts** – *C6* – *1111 SW Broadway Ave.* – *Box office:* 📞 *(800) 273 1530* – *www.portland5.com.* This important institution manages the three venues in the building, including the **Newmark Theatre**, and two other venues a stone's throw away:

② **Keller Auditorium** – *C6* – *222 SW Clay St.* – ♿.

③ **Arlene Schnitzer Concert Hall** – *C6* – *1037 SW Broadway Ave.* – ♿. Companies and orchestras that perform at these venues:

Oregon Ballet Theatre – 📞 *(503) 222 5538* – *www.obt.org.* This ballet company presents six shows per season. Discover their classic and contemporary pieces at the Keller Auditorium and Newmark Theatre.

Portland Opera – 📞 *(503) 241 1802* – *www.portlandopera.org.* The Keller Auditorium, as part of Portland'5 Centers for the Arts, is *the* venue for Portland opera.

Oregon Symphony – 📞 *(503) 228 1353* – *www.orsymphony.org.* Founded in 1896, this orchestra performs the great classics and popular music at the Arlene Schnitzer Concert Hall.

④ **Artists Repertory Theatre** – *B5* – *1515 SW Morrison St.* – 📞 *(503) 241 1278* – *www.artistsrep.org* – 🅿 ♿. The resident actors of this company present classic and contemporary productions throughout the season, in cozy venues.

⑤ **Portland Center Stage at The Armory** – *C5* – *128 NW 11ᵗʰ Ave.* – 📞 *(503) 445 3700* – *www.pcs.org* – ♿. The Gerding Theater and Ellyn Bye Studio are two performance halls for large and small productions.

ROCK, POP AND FOLK VENUES

⑥ **Crystal Ballroom** – *C5* – *1332 W Burnside St.* – 📞 *(503) 225 0047* – *www.crystalballroompdx.com.* Built in 1914 as a ballroom, this venue puts on a varied program ranging from folk music to head-banging rock. The third floor of the building, opened in the 1980s, has resplendent murals on the walls, glimmering chandeliers and sky-high ceilings.

7 Wonder Ballroom – *D3* – *128 NE Russell St. – ☎ (503) 284 8686 – www.wonderballroom.com – ♿ – Prices and opening hours depend on concerts.* Also built in 1914, this distinguished historical building in the Northeast houses one of the main venues in town. Here you'll find an eclectic program, from blues and hip hop to electro rock.

8 Mississippi Studios – *C2* – *3939 N Mississippi Ave. – ☎ (503) 288 3895 – www.mississippistudios.com – 11am–2am.* This temple of independent music is a bar, restaurant and concert hall all rolled into one. Here you really get an idea of Portland's non-conformist spirit while soaking up the contagious energy of the Northeast. There's a fairly specialized rock and folk-pop program and a relaxed atmosphere.

9 Revolution Hall – *D5* – *1300 SE Stark St. – ☎ (503) 288 3895 – www.revolutionhall.com – 11am–2am.* Housed in a former high school built in 1924, this concert hall used to be the school auditorium, complete with original wooden seats. There's an eclectic program of mainly pop and folk music.

10 Aladdin Theater – *D7* – *3017 SE Milwaukie Ave. – ☎ (503) 234 9694 – www.aladdin-theater.com – 🅿 ♿ Contact in advance.* In Southeast, this 620-seat venue, formerly a boulevard theater, has preserved something of its 1920s style. Famous for its excellent acoustics, on the program you'll find jazz, blues, pop and world music.

MUSIC HALL

11 Darcelle XV – *C5* – *208 NW 3rd Ave. – ☎ (503) 222 5338 – darcellexv.com – Tue 6pm–9:30pm, Tue–Thur 6pm–11pm, (2am Fri–Sat).* An eclectic institution right at the heart of Old Town, this nightclub puts on drag queen playback concerts where the MCs wear staggering stiletto heels and reign over an exuberant atmosphere. Here you're sure to experience a kooky, queer and unforgettably hilarious night.

ARCADES

12 Ground Kontrol – *C5* – *115 NW 5th Ave. – ☎ (503) 796 9364 – groundkontrol.com – Noon–2am.* Play arcade games from the afternoon into the wee hours surrounded by neon 80s decor at this Old Town hangout, where the cocktails are very sweet.

13 Avalon Theatre & Wunderland – *F6* – *3451 SE Belmont St. – ☎ (503) 238 1617 – wunderlandgames.com – Noon–midnight (11am Sat).* Another Portland arcade temple, this wonderland of pinball machines and video games is yet more retro, and also has a family atmosphere.

Where to stay

Hotel offerings in Portland have developed in recent years but is still concentrated mainly in **Downtown, Old Town** and **the Pearl District**, with their trendy, elegant and generally expensive hotels. This location is ideal for guests to make the most of museums and restaurants, and to get around without the need for a car or taxis. There are fewer options on the **Eastside**, but they are slightly cheaper and let you enjoy the bohemian and relaxed atmosphere of the "real" districts where most Portlanders live today. If you choose this option, note that you'll have to use public transport or bikes, or take a taxi or car service, to access neighborhoods across the city.

Find the addresses on the detachable map (inside the cover) using the number in the listing (for example ①). The coordinates in red (for example D2) refer to the same map.

DOWNTOWN

$150–400

② **Dossier** – *C5* – *750 SW Alder St. – ☎ (503) 294 9000 – www.dossier hotel.com –* ♿ *– 205 rooms –* ✕. Luxe and trendy, this lovely hotel brings together the edgy charm of Downtown and the service of a first-class hotel. The carefully designed, modern rooms are equipped with beds that are so comfortable you won't want to get up in the morning. The hotel's bar-restaurant Opel is famous for its cocktails and there's a bike hire service, a valet, and umbrellas to borrow (they come in handy in Portland).

④ **Ace Hotel** – *C5* – *1022 SW Stark St. – ☎ (503) 228 2277 – www.acehotel.com – 79 rooms –* ✕. An excellent boutique hotel with vintage signs, glamorous staff and bikes to rent. From the communal areas to the guestrooms, you'll find arty, chic and pared-back decor (salvaged furniture, murals, sliding wooden panels instead of doors, etc.).

⑤ **The Benson Hotel** – *C5* – *309 SW Broadway – ☎ (503) 228 2000 – www.coasthotels.com –* ▦ ⓟ *For a fee –* ♿ *– 287 rooms –* ✕. Timber baron Simon Benson built this hotel in 1913 and its opulence has endured through the ages. Sophisticated chandeliers of Austrian crystal light up the marble floors and walnut paneling. The guestrooms are understated and elegant, offering every modern comfort.

③ **Hotel Lucia** – *C5* – *400 SW Broadway – ☎ (503) 225 1717 – hotellucia.com –* ⓟ *For a fee –* ♿ *– 128 rooms.* A lovely hotel where the attention to detail makes for a wonderful stay: the radio comes on as you enter the room, creating a warm feel, and conversations can be struck up over a free pint of local beer, served every day from 5-6pm. There is a gym and a bike rental service.

⑧ **Hotel Zags** – *C6* – *515 SW Clay St. – ☎ (503) 484 1084 – www. thehotelzags.com –* ▦ ⓟ *For a fee –* ♿ *– 174 rooms –* ✕. This fancy boutique hotel marries 1950s style and modern comforts. The rooms are all simple with touches of color and are completed with contemporary artworks by local artists. The Nel Centro restaurant serves up affordable dishes inspired by French and Italian cuisine using local products.

$250–650

6 Sentinel Hotel – *C5* – 614 SW 11th Ave. – ☏ (503) 224 3400 – www.sentinelhotel.com – ▤ ▯ For a fee – 100 rooms – ✕. Murals evoke Lewis and Clark's 19th-century expedition and original features from 1909 include the stained-glass dome and tiled floors. Handsome mahogany elements are found throughout. The rooms are large and modern.

9 The Heathman Hotel – *C6* – 1001 SW Broadway – ☏ (503) 241 4100 – heathmanhotel.com – ▯ For a fee – ♿ – 150 rooms – ✕. Portland's iconic luxury hotel, built in 1927, exudes Old World elegance. The rooms, which have all modern conveniences, are fitted with dark wooden furniture that enhances the pale gold walls, decorated with original art from the Northwest. The hotel's motto is very fitting: "Here, service is still an art." Seafood restaurant Headwaters (☕ Where to eat) has a menu of local dishes.

10 RiverPlace Hotel – *C6* – 1510 SW Harbor Way – ☏ (503) 228 3233 – www.riverplacehotel.com – ▯ For a fee – ♿ – 85 rooms – ✕. This Kimpton Group hotel perches on the banks of the Willamette. The chic, welcoming rooms have wide windows providing splendid views over the river. Although very near the center, the

hotel makes you feel as though you've escaped the bustle of the city. As for the restaurant, its name gives a clue to what might be on the menu: King Tide Fish & Shell showcases the delights of the sea.

7 The Nines – *C5* – 525 SW Morrison St. – ☏ (877) 229 9995 – www.thenines.com – ▤ ▯ For a fee – ♿ – 331 rooms – ✕. On the top floors of an old department store at the heart of Downtown, The Nines has gained recognition for its contemporary discreet luxury. Taupe wallpaper enhanced with ivory-colored floral patterns, crystal chandeliers and modern art by local artists decorate the rooms. The sumptuous linen and thick armchairs only add to the comfort. Located in the several-story-high lobby, the restaurant Urban Farmer specializes in grass-fed Oregon beef.

OLD TOWN/CHINATOWN

$100–300

11 The Society Hotel – *C5* – 203 NW 3rd Ave. – ☏ (503) 445 0444 – thesocietyhotel.com – ▤ ♿ – 60 rooms. This former boarding house for sailors (1881) in Chinatown has been transformed into a hipster-style hotel that provides good value for money. There is a café in the entrance hall and a rooftop terrace is perfect for a cocktail with a view. It's an attractive option in the center of Portland. As well as the clean and modern rooms and suites that feature rustic brick walls, shared dorm rooms are also available.

14 **The Hoxton Portland** – *C5* – *15 NW 4th Ave.* – *(503) 770 0500* – *thehoxton.com* – 🖥 ♿ – *119 rooms* – ✖️. The latest from the trendy British group The Hoxton is set in a sumptuous historical building in a prime location right next to Chinatown Gate. It has two restaurants: Lovely Rita (♿ *Where to eat*) and Tope (♿ *Where to drink*), a discreet speakeasy that's one of the best bars in town, with a stylish, international clientèle. The larger guestrooms come with a price tag to match.

NORTHWEST DISTRICT

$170–300

1 **Inn at Northrup Station** – *B4* – *2025 NW Northrup St.* – *(503) 224 0543* – *www.northrupstation.com* – 🖥 🅿 ♿ – *70 rooms.* Lime green, brilliant purple and other bright colors welcome guests to this boutique hotel in the fashionable district of Nob Hill. The bedrooms, decorated with zeal, have small kitchens equipped with maple cupboards and granite counters. There are contemporary artworks throughout. The establishment provides tram tickets to its guests for free, the closest stop being right outside the hotel's entrance. They also offer bikes.

CENTRAL EASTSIDE

$170–300

12 **Jupiter Hotel** – *D5* – *800 E Burnside St.* – *(503) 230 9200* – *jupiterhotel.com* – 🖥 🅿 *For a fee* – *81 rooms* – *2 nights min. on weekends during high season.* – ✖️. This is a revamped American motel with 1950s vintage decor, minimalist bedrooms and a sophisticated pared-back look. This chic but discreet style is very Portland. There's a friendly rock atmosphere at the bar-restaurant-concert hall Doug Fir Lounge, which is like a large log cabin with retro furnishings. There are frequent concerts here featuring local rock bands. The hotel also offers bikes.

15 **Jupiter NEXT** – *D5* – *900 E Burnside St.* – *(503) 230 9200* – *jupiterhotel.com* – 🖥 – *67 rooms* – ✖️. Modern and extremely comfortable rooms, a fantastic view over the city, a trendy bar-restaurant (Hey Love, ♿see *Where to eat*), and an

Doug Fir Lounge, Jupiter Hotel

Photo by NashCO/Travel Portland

ideal location between the historical center and the bohemian east: Jupiter's older brother and neighbor has everything going for it. More contemporary and design-focused than Jupiter, it's also full of charm and not in any way imposing. Like its sibling, this hotel also offers bikes.

NORTHEAST

$165–175

13 **Caravan** – *D1* – *5009 NE 11th Ave. – ✆ (503) 288 5225 – tinyhousehotel. com – 6 caravans.* To the northeast of Downtown in a trendy district with many bars and restaurants is this atypical hotel in an urban setting. Stay in modest but stylish tiny homes set out around a communal area with tables, deck chairs and seats. Fitted with showers and small kitchens, these caravans house two to four people. Despite their small size they're a fun alternative to traditional hotels.

COLUMBIA RIVER GORGE NATIONAL SCENIC AREA

Around $200

Hood River Hotel – *102 Oak St. – Hood River – ✆ (541) 386 1900 – www. hoodriverhotel.com.* At the heart of the lively and just-a-tad trendy small town of Hood River, this hotel was initially conceived in 1912 as an annex to a larger hotel that no longer exists. Following a complete revamp in 2017, it has a strong vintage look, its foyer dominated by a lovely chimney and its large rooms decorated in shades

of gray. The rooms range from single bedrooms to family apartments with bedrooms and kitchens. Tuck in to a Scandinavian breakfast at Broder Øst.

AROUND MOUNT HOOD

Around $250

Timberline Lodge – *27500 E Timberline Rd – Government Camp – ✆ (503) 272 3311 – www. timberlinelodge.com.* Entering this huge building, you'll find yourself in a maze of corridors and rooms, where the smell of wood fires in the fireplace hints at this hotel's history (**¿** *p. 53*). The palatial lounge with its period furniture invites you to relax and take in the splendor of Mount Hood (except in the depths of winter, when 30-foot snow piles can block the view!). There are small and large rooms and you can also stay in dorms. The swimming pool, which opens in the evenings and is heated year round, is definitely a bonus, as is the excellent restaurant. It's an Oregon experience not to be missed!

WILLAMETTE VALLEY

$265–720

Black Walnut Inn – *960 NE Worden Hill Rd – Dundee – ✆ (503) 433 2715 – www.blackwalnutvineyard.com –* **P** *– 9 rooms – ⌷.* Experience the great pleasure of sleeping at this beautiful winery. This large, yellow-walled country house—a replica of a Tuscan property—has classically decorated, elegant and comfortable rooms. There are large bathrooms and balconies with views out over the vineyard. A gourmet breakfast and wine tasting is included.

Around $500

The Allison Inn & Spa – *2525 Allison Lane - Newberg* – ✆ *(503) 554 2525* – *www.theallison.com* – 🅿 🛌 ♿ – *77 rooms* – ✕. This hotel, nestled amidst Oregon's vineyards, is a modern and luxurious chalet that will delight wine enthusiasts visiting the Willamette Valley. The inn is LEED Gold certified for its compliance with environmental standards. The neutral-toned rooms are furnished with high-quality linens, original works of art, and windows that open out onto the hillside or vineyards. A spa and swimming pool just add to the luxurious nature of the inn. The restaurant, Jory, combines local fare with a wine list featuring 800 wines.

MCMINNVILLE

$105–720

Hotel Oregon – *310 NE Evans St.* – ✆ *(503) 472 8427* – *www. mcmenamins.com* – *42 rooms* – ✕. A former bus depot, this 1905 brick building has undergone a spectacular transformation. Today it's a welcoming meeting point and hotel historically linked to the vineyards. There's a pub on the first floor, one great bar in the basement and a second on the rooftop. The Paragon Room is a billiards room by day and a concert hall by night. You can find clues to the establishment's history in the photographs and early 20th century

decor. The rooms are spacious, furnished with chenille bed covers and vintage wardrobes. Some rooms share a bathroom.

$200–400

Youngberg Hill – *10660 SW Youngberg Hill Rd* – ✆ *(503) 472 2727* – *youngberghill.com.* Follow the narrow, winding road that climbs the vine-carpeted hill. At the very top is this lovely house, owned by the eponymous winery, a haven of peace and tranquility with very comfortable rooms, all with a view over the countryside and vineyard. A charming spot at the heart of the Willamette Valley!

OREGON COAST

Over $300

Cannery Pier Hotel – *10 Basin St.* – ✆ *(503) 325 4996* – *www. cannerypierhotel.com* – *46 rooms and suites* – ☕. On the site of the former Union Fish Cannery, this modern hotel has been built 600 feet into the Columbia River. Historical photographs and the boats passing close to the hotel both add to its unique atmosphere. The bedrooms, decorated in taupe, open out onto balconies. The town used to be populated by Finns and the breakfast includes Finnish specialties, while the spa has a Finnish sauna.

Planning your trip

Know before you go

101

Basic information

Festivals and cultural events

Cycle Portland bike tour, Pearl District
© Jamie Francis/Travel Portland

Know before you go

ARRIVING BY PLANE

Prices vary depending on the season and airline. Prices skyrocket during Northern Hemisphere summer vacation.

Airlines
There are direct flights to Portland (PDX) from many US cities and from Vancouver and connecting flights from other international destinations. Airlines that fly to Portland include Air Canada; Air France; Alaska, American; British Airways; Condor; Delta; JetBlue, KLM; Southwest, United; and WestJet.

Luggage
Be aware that if you have a **layover** in the US to take a connecting flight, you will have to go through immigration, pick up your luggage, go through security and check your bags for the domestic flight. Border security can take a long time because the large airports can be very busy; at PDX, ranked number one for US airports, lines move relatively quickly. To make sure you don't miss your flight, leave at least 1.5hrs for the layover. For the return journey, you can check your luggage through to your final destination.
All checked luggage is subject to examination by the **Transport Security Administration** (TSA), which has the right to open bags if it is deemed necessary. If you lock your suitcases, make sure you use a TSA-approved lock, otherwise it may be broken open.

You should arrive at the airport 1.5-2h in advance to allow time to pass through security.

Security
Security measures for flights to or from the US are extremely strict. No **liquids**, aerosols, gels, pastes or creams over 3oz/100ml are permitted in the cabin. They should be in a single transparent, ziploc plastic bag of 1 quart or less. Baby food, liquid medication (with relevant prescription) and liquids bought in duty free (in a sealed bag with the receipt shown) are allowed. Some **medications** (notably narcotics) cannot be taken through customs. If you bring medicine with you, make sure you bring your prescription.
One quart of alcohol per person over 21, 200 cigarettes and 50 cigars may be **imported** into the US, as can gifts worth $100 or less.

Arriving in the US
At border and immigration control, your fingerprints and photo may be taken and you may be asked a series of questions by an immigration officer. Answer seriously even if some of the questions seem irrelevant.

US citizens and Canadian visitors can use the Mobile Passport app at 27 airports in the US, including Portland (see *www.cbp.gov/travel/us-citizens/mobile-passport-control*). This really speeds up entry into the US.
🚆 *By train and by bus, p. 3.*

PORTLAND KNOWS NO BOUNDS.
NEITHER DO YOU.

Discover a new side of America and visit Portland, with Delta's nonstop service from London Heathrow, and stay connected to what matters thanks to Wi-Fi and free messaging available on Delta flights.

BORDER CONTROL

Check your passport **before booking your travel**: if it has expired or if you need a visa, you will need extra time to renew or apply. If in doubt, consult the US embassy: **usembassy.gov**.

Passport
To enter the United States without a visa, visitors (including children) must have a valid **biometric** passport (issued since 2009).
Children, no matter their age, must have an individual passport: the US authorities do not recognize children being added to their parents' passports.

Visa
Visas are not required for citizens of 38 countries, including Australia, Canada, the UK, Ireland, and New Zealand, who visit as tourists for stays of less than 90 days. However, they are required for study or professional activity in the US. See *travel.state.gov/content/travel/en/us-visas/tourism-visit/visa-waiver-program.html*

ESTA
Travelers who do not need a visa must have a round-trip plane or cruise ticket and fill in a **request for electronic travel authorization** (**ESTA**) at least 72hr before departure (and preferably further in advance). To do so, fill in the online form at **esta.cbp.dhs.gov** (the ONLY official website; avoid other search engine results).
The authorization, which remains valid for multiple entries over two years, costs $14, payable online by credit or debit card. You should receive a response from the site within a few hours, and possibly immediately. Once you have received authorization, it is a good idea to print a confirmation to have a record of your reference number. If your request is rejected, you should apply for a visa from the consulate.

CALLING THE US

To call the US or Canada from abroad, dial 00 + 1 + the 10 digit telephone number. You *only* need 00 *if* you're calling from a landline. 👋 *Phones, p. 114.*

INSURANCE

Don't skimp on health insurance as costs can soar very quickly, particularly for scans and hospitalization. Check with your credit card company, because cards provide coverage abroad. If your insurance at home does not cover you abroad, buy travel health insurance. **www.travelinsurance.com** and **www.insuremytrip.com** are good sites for comparing travel insurance plans and costs.
Make sure you check the terms carefully. How much is the deductible? How much is covered? You should request coverage of at least US$150,000. 👋 *Health, p. 110.*

TOURIST INFORMATION

Oregon – www.travelportland.com; www.traveloregon.com; www.facebook.com/TravelOregon; www.portlandoregon.gov.

© DaveAlan/iStockphoto.com

Mount Hood viewed from Portland International Airport

US – www.visittheusa.com; www. facebook.com/VisitTheUSA/

WEATHER

Seasons
Portland has a coastal climate. The best time to visit is from **May to September**, when it's sunniest and temperatures are comparable to the Mediterranean.

Fall is wetter, but still spectacular, as the lush natural surroundings come alive with color.

The winters, which can be long, gray and rainy, are still generally mild, especially if you come from a colder climate.

Weather forecasts
See **www.weather.com** and **www. accuweather.com**.

Basic information

ALCOHOL

You must be at least **21 years old** to buy and consume alcohol. You can buy alcohol in liquor stores and beer and wine in grocery stores. As a rule, you shouldn't carry open bottles inside your car or drink openly in public areas.

When driving, the maximum alcohol level permitted is 0.8% (considerably less than in some other countries).

DATE AND TIME

Dates

In the United States, the **date** is written with the month first, then the day and then the year. For example, May 11, 2019 would be 05/11/19.

Time

The **time** is given with a number from 1 to 12 followed by am *(ante meridiem)* for the morning and pm *(post meridiem)* for the afternoon or evening: 8am is 8 o'clock in the morning, while 8pm is 8 o'clock in the evening (20:00 military time). Similarly, 12am is midnight and 12pm is noon.

Time zones

The United States has four time zones. Bear this in mind if you have to take connecting flights in the US. **Oregon** is on **Pacific Standard Time** (PST), which is GMT-8 hours.

CULTURAL TIPS

Americans, like Brits, form orderly **lines**. Cutting a queue is considered rude.

In most **restaurants**, you should wait to be seated rather than sitting immediately down at a table. This is usually indicated on a sign at the entrance of the restaurant.

Americans can be very friendly and warm, striking up conversations and chatting to people at the next table at a restaurant or cafe. Politically, America is a country divided. Portland itself is a prime example of this: a liberal bastion in a conservative state. Unless you know someone well, it's easiest to avoid any criticism of US domestic and foreign policy. This will only make things awkward. For example, it's best not to bring up topics like **abortion**, the **death penalty** or **gun ownership**, unless you are sure that you are on the same page as the person you're talking to. Many people are horrified and angered by the current US administration and would rather discuss happier things. The same goes for **religion**. Some Americans find it important. Don't be surprised if you meet someone and are almost immediately asked what you do for work. This is a common topic in America, where work and social success are essential values.

CYCLING

In Portland, cyclists rule the roads, and the bike lanes make you feel completely safe as you ride, even in bustling Downtown. Cycling along the banks of the Willamette and exploring the city's outskirts and surrounding area is a great experience. The tourist office has a free map of the bike lanes.
& *Map of bike lanes on the reverse side of the detachable map.*
You'll find bike rental services in many hotels and bike shops.
Biketown – www.biketownpdx.com. A self-service bike system with 1,000 bikes and 125 stations throughout the city. There's a sign-up fee of $5, then a usage charge of $0.08 per minute. Unfortunately, the service doesn't always work that well.
& *Guided tours, p. 110.*

DRIVING

To drive, you'll need a driver's license that is over a year old (good for up to a three-month stay). It's not mandatory to have an international license. The same goes for motorcycle licenses.

Car rental

To rent a car, the driver should be at least 21 years old. Car rental companies only take credit card payments (Visa or Mastercard). The main rental companies can be found at the Portland airport, but you should book online to get the best price.
Alamo – www.alamo.com; **Avis** – www.avis.com; **Budget** – www.budget.com; **Dollar** – www.dollar.com;

Enterprise – www.enterprise.com; **Hertz** – www.hertz.com; **National** – www.nationalcar.com; **Thrifty** – www.thrifty.com.

Driving

Almost all cars have **automatic transmission**: D to drive, R to reverse, P for park, N for neutral and L or M for a low gear (1st or 2nd) for tackling hills.

The rules of the road

Take note of the **speed limits** (which vary between states). On interstate highways, the speed limit is 70 mph. If there is no speed limit is given, it's usually 55 or 65 mph on rural highways, 20 to 35 mph in cities and 15 mph in school zones (to be strictly observed).
You shouldn't pass a school bus when its warning lights are flashing.
Obey the stop signs at all intersections. Except where prohibited by a sign, you can **turn right at a red light**, after first making sure the way is clear.
In the city, there are central left turn lanes in the middle of the road.

Gas

Gas is sold by the gallon with the price varying between states and by town. At the time of writing, a gallon cost roughly $3.38 in Oregon. Except in small towns, it is illegal in Oregon to pump your own gas. A gas station attendant will do it for you; there is no extra cost for this, and you do not tip.

ELECTRICITY

In the United States, standard voltage is **110 V** and plugs have two flat parallel pins. You can get voltage converters to change the current from 220 V to 110 V (check before traveling). Bring an **adapter** with you or buy one in a supermarket.

FOOD AND DRINK

Breakfast
Usually served from 7am until 11–11:30am (or even all day) **breakfast** is sizable and usually good value for money (allow $5 to $15 depending on the number of dishes). At the weekend, most restaurants offer **brunch**.

Lunch
Lunch is the lightest meal of the day and is served until after 3pm. Allow $4 to $9 for a **sandwich**, often served with fries, a salad or soup. Another option is one of the huge prepared **salads** (Caesar salad, chopped salad, etc.), or the make-your-own versions you can get at salad bars (from $6 to $12). **Food carts** (♿ p. 132) are a great option if you want to grab something to eat on-the-go. They have very affordable and often delicious menus. Most restaurants and bars have a **lunch menu** with one-dish meals that are similar to, but slightly smaller and a lot cheaper than, those served for dinner ($8 to $15).

Happy hour
Portland is the capital of this US tradition, which gives you the chance to try pricey restaurant cuisine for much less than at dinner. From around 4:30pm to 6pm, there is often a reduced menu with up to 50% off select items. Some restaurants also have a happy hour from 9:30pm until they close.

Dinner
Dinner hour varies across the US but is earlier than in Europe. In Portland, where there is a lively nightlife, the restaurants close later (last orders often at 9:30pm).
Dinner is usually the largest meal of the day: these can be the same dishes as lunchtime, but with larger portions and a higher price. For foodies, this is the moment to sample the most refined restaurants. The **menu** is divided into three main sections. Also called appetizers, the starters usually consist of one dish ($7 to $15). The main dish is also called an entrée ($15 to $30). Desserts are huge and usually very sweet ($6 to $10).

Drinks
Some chain and family restaurants don't serve alcohol as they need a special license (a wine license for wines or full license for all types of alcohol). High-quality establishments have extensive **wine lists** (often featuring excellent Oregon wines). These can be expensive, but can often be ordered by the glass.
Generally, once seated, you'll be served a glass of iced tap water which is topped up during the meal. This is free. Mineral water is not often served and, as it is often imported, it can be expensive. In Portland, it's all the rage to drink **alternative beverages**, which are almost always artisanal: cider, kombucha (a fermented, nonalcoholic drink), and kava (a drink from the Pacific Islands believed to have calming properties) are gradually replacing sodas that some Americans drink with their meals.

travelplanners
service beyond the call

travelplanners are the UK's leading operator for high-quality, great value holidays. Our experienced, well-travelled advisors look after you with great attention to detail and personal care, ensuring your expectations are met at all times.

Explore Portland from £1035 per person

Affectionately referred to as "City of Roses" Portland is famous for many things including a fantastic culinary scene, the welcoming locals, an amazing public transportation system that includes cycle friendly streets, historic monuments and museums, a lively arts and culture scene and much more - all surrounded by some spectacular countryside and wilderness just waiting to be explored.

3 Nights	**The Benson Hotel, Portland**
2 Nights	**Embassy Suites Washington Square, Tualatin Valley**
2 Nights	**Best Western Plus Rivershore Inn, Oregon City, Oregon's Mount Hood Territory**

Call 020 3542 8888 for more details or visit our website www.travelplanners.co.uk

ABTA
Travel with confidence
ABTA No. L5556

3085 ATOL PROTECTED

2019 Gold Trusted Service feefo

At some restaurants, a refill is included in the price of your drink.

In the bars, opt for **craft beers** rather than the domestic brands (Coors, Budweiser, Michelob, etc.). Portland is teeming with microbreweries (♿ *p. 81*) with refined offerings. You can also order draft beer (on tap).

GUIDED TOURS

Walking tours

Portland Walking Tours – Departure from the Portland Walking Tours office, Pioneer Square: 701 SW 6th Ave. – ℘ (503) 774 4522 – portlandwalkingtours.com. Choose between several different themes to discover Portland: cultural ($23), underground (♿ *p. 26*), ghost tour ($19), etc. Indulge in some delicious food on the food cart tour (♿ *p. 66*).

Architectural Heritage Center – 701 SE Grand Ave. – ℘ (503) 231 7264 – visitahc.org – Duration 2hr – $20. They offer guided tours of Portland's architecture: the bridges, Northwest Broadway, Old Town, etc. See web for full program and to register.

Cycling

Cycle Portland – Departure 117 NW 2nd Ave. – ℘ 844 739 2453 – www.portlandbicycletours.com. Portland is particularly well suited for guided bike tours. There are three options: the Portland city tour ($39), microbreweries tour ($49) and culinary tour ($59).

By bus

Gray Line of Portland – Departs from 525 SW Naito Pkwy – ℘ (503) 710 4391 – graylineofportland.com. They offer a hop-on hop-off pink trolley sightseeing tour ($37) and Multnomah Falls and Columbia River Gorge tour ($59).

By boat

Portland Spirit – Departure 1020 SW Naito Pkwy – ℘ (503) 224 3900 – www.portlandspirit.com. Cruise on the Willamette (about 2hr – $32 without a meal, from $48 with a meal).

By helicopter

Oregon Helicopters – Departure from the heliport on the roof of 33 NW Davis St. – ℘ (503) 987 0060 – oregonhelicopters.com. This is an incredible experience; fly over Portland's skyscrapers (5min – $59) or parks (10min – $79), above Downtown (15min – $119) or over the Willamette falls (20min – $175).

HEALTH

In an emergency, call 911 or head to the nearest hospital, but bear in mind that emergency services can often be extremely costly. If it's not a life-threatening problem, you can get a **walk-in consultation** (where you can see a doctor without an appointment) at a **walk-in clinic** or a **doctor's office**. Without insurance, it will cost a minimum of $150, not including treatment. ♿ *Insurance, p. 104.*

Pharmacies

Medicines, prescription and over the counter, are sold at **drugstores** and **pharmacies**. Most corner stores and supermarkets also have a medicine aisle.

Emergencies

Dial **911** no matter where you are.

INTERNET

Travelers will find it easy to get online almost anywhere. Most hotels and motels have free **WiFi**. Many hotels also have a business center with computers where you can use the internet for free, while B&Bs often have a computer that can be used by guests. WiFi is also free for customers in restaurants, bars, cafés, fast-food restaurants and some public spaces.

MAIL

www.usps.com – US Postal Service. **Central Post Office** – *C4* – 715 NW Hoyt St. In Pearl District, near the train station. **Stamps** are sold in post offices: $1.15 for an international postcard or letter weighing less than 1 oz. A domestic postcard stamp costs 35 cents; a domestic letter costs 55 cents.

MEDIA

The two most popular daily papers are the **Washington Post** and the **New York Times**. Common weekly news magazines are **Time** and **Newsweek**. The **Oregonian** is the main daily paper in the state. **Willamette Week** is a weekly paper with local news and event and entertainment listings. The magazine **Bitch**, which campaigns for feminism and provides a thoughtful, bold critique of mass culture, is based in Portland. Portland's artistic and intellectual community publishes many interesting **fanzines** that can be found at Powell's (👆 p. 88) and other independent bookstores.
See television channel KATU, based in Portland, for local news – www.katu.com.
You can also pick up international newspapers in Portland.

MONEY

The US currency is the **dollar** ($), divided into 100 cents.
There are 1, 5, 10, 20, 50 and 100-dollar bills, and coins of 1 cent (penny), 5 cents (nickel), 10 cents (dime), 25 cents (quarter), 50 cents (half dollar) and $1. All the coins are silvery, apart from the 1-cent coin (copper) and the $1 coin (golden and not too common). Be careful: the bills look similar as they are all green and the same size. Note that the 10-cent coin is smaller than the 5-cent one.

Currency exchange

Most national bank branches offer currency exchange, charging a moderate commission. The best exchange rate will be found taking money out of an ATM.

Cash

There are **ATMs** everywhere, even in some shops, restaurants and grocery stores. ATMs not belonging to your bank will charge a fee of $1-4. To ensure your card doesn't get blocked, make sure you stay within your maximum daily or weekly withdrawal limits.

Wonders of Portland & Beyond

11 nights from **£2,479**

Direct flights, car hire incl a free upgrade, 3★ to 4★
accommodation and Mt St Helens Monument Tour

- *Historic and modern architecture of Portland*
- *Rugged coastlines • Crater Lake National Park*
- *Columbia River Gorge • Charming seaside towns*
- *Impressive forts & numerous craft breweries*

Tailormade Travel Worldwide   **020 7368 1506**
First & Business Class Travel   **020 7938 0213**

trailfinders.com

Credit cards

Almost all credit cards are accepted. These are essential when it comes to booking a hotel room or renting a car. Use a credit card with no foreign transaction fees. The exchange rate from the day of the transaction will be applied. When you use your card to pay in a **store**, you'll be asked: debit or credit? Foreign cards will always be considered credit cards even when they are actually debit. You will have to sign the receipt and won't need to enter your PIN.

Visa – ☎ 1 303 967 1096 (from a landline). If you lose your card, call this number.

In an emergency, you can send or receive money immediately using: **Western Union** – ☎ 1 800 325 6000 (from the US) – www.westernunion.com.

OPENING HOURS

Government buildings, **banks** and **post offices** are usually open from Monday to Friday, 9am to 5pm, and often on Saturday mornings (except for government buildings).

Stores usually close around 6pm, although large shopping malls often stay open until 8pm or 9pm, and corner stores or bodegas may stay open until 11pm or later. On Sundays, many are open from 1–2pm to 5–6pm. Hypermarts like Target and Fred Meyer are open daily until 10pm or later.

PHONES

Local and domestic calls

US phone numbers are composed of an **area code** with 3 digits - **503, 541, and 971** for Oregon - followed by the 7-digit number of the person you're contacting.

For example, if you want to call Visit Portland and you're already in the US, dial 503-427-1372. If you were outside the US, you'd dial +1 before the area code 503. For calls local and to other states, dial the area code, then the rest of the phone number.

Toll-free numbers

Numbers starting with 800, 877, 888, 866 are free to call (they are always marked as toll-free). They can also be called from outside the US, but if they are, they will incur a fee.

If you need to call one of these numbers, dial 1 first if you're calling from a landline (not necessary if you're calling from a cell phone).

Information

To reach an operator, dial ☎ 411 (local numbers), 555 1212 (intercity numbers), or (1) 800 874 4000, and 324 from a landline (international numbers).

Calls

Use your phone or computer to make free or inexpensive calls (local and international) on Skype, Google Hangouts, or Whatsapp. You'll need data or WiFi, but this is widely available.

Hotels – Avoid making international calls from your room, as the rates are extortionate.

Cell phones – Cell phones should be tri-band or quad-band rather than dual-band to work in the USA. If your phone is not American, activate the

international service option before leaving home. Make sure, however, that you deactivate the "data roaming" option, as well as 3G or 4G service (use WiFi for internet), otherwise you'll get a huge bill. Don't forget to set up the access code to your voicemail before you leave so that you can listen to your messages.

You can buy an American **SIM card** to use in your cell phone if it is unlocked. You'll receive a local phone number and credit for a certain amount of minutes and/or data. You can buy SIM cards at phone stores; T-Mobile is a good option. Top them up online and at supermarkets, drugstores or gas stations.

Prepaid cell phone – You can buy these at any phone store. You buy the phone and the plan (they start at around $30), which you then top-up with codes that you can buy online and at supermarkets, bodegas, post offices and newspaper stands. Warning: both outgoing and incoming calls incur a charge.

PUBLIC HOLIDAYS AND SCHOOL VACATIONS

Public holidays
New Year's Day – January 1.
Martin Luther King Day – 3rd Monday in January.
Presidents' Day* – 3rd Monday in February, in honor of US presidents.
Memorial Day – Last Monday of May, to remember war victims.
Independence Day – July 4, national holiday commemorating the founding of the US.

Labor Day – 1st Monday of September, holiday celebrating workers.
Columbus Day* – 2nd Monday of October, the day that Christopher Columbus "discovered" America.
Veterans Day – November 11, commemorating veterans (Armistice Day).
Thanksgiving – 4th Thursday of November, a celebration of family and good fortune.
Christmas Day – December 25.
*Government offices and banks may be closed but shops and restaurants will be open.

School vacations
Dates vary from state to state and county to county, but generally speaking, they are the following:
Summer vacation – From late May (Memorial Day) to early September (Labor Day).
Fall break – Around Thanksgiving, the last week of November.
Christmas vacation – Shortly before Christmas until a few days after January 1.
Spring break – A week around the Easter weekend.

PUBLIC TRANSPORTATION

In Portland
TriMet MAX Light Rail and Buses – ☏ (503) 238 7433 – www.trimet. org/max. Portland is known for its excellent transportation system. One key element is the **light rail**, whose 60 miles of tracks link the town, airport, and surrounding areas. In town, the **five lines** run every day

with an average frequency of one train every 15min. A ticket valid for 2hr30min costs $2.50 (a day pass costs $5) and can be bought from the ticket machines at light rail stops.
Portland Streetcar – ℘ (503) 238 7433 – www.portlandstreetcar. org – Mon–Fri 5:30am–11:30pm, Sat 7:30am–11:30pm, Sun 7:30am–10:30pm. The **streetcar** is efficient for getting around the city. There are **two lines**: one from north to south across the city center, and the other a loop crossing the Willamette River. Streetcars run every 15min. A ticket valid for 2hr30min costs $2.50. You can buy it on the streetcar or at any of the stops. The same ticket is valid on all public transit (lightrail, bus and streetcar). ♿ *Transport map on the reverse side of the detachable map.*

Getting to the surrounding area
Greyhound – ℘ 800 231 2222 – www.greyhound.com. The first bus company in the US connects almost all US towns and small municipalities. Buses are a bit dated but relatively inexpensive.

SAFETY

Portland is a relatively safe city. However, as in all large cities, you should be careful. Over the last few years, the Old Town district has become a refuge for hundreds of homeless people, because there are shelters there providing food and support. They rarely bother passers-by, are generally friendly and always appreciate a kind gesture. So, if you can't finish your copious restaurant meal, ask for a take-away box and cutlery and give it to someone in need. It will be a small act that makes a big difference.

SHOPPING

The US is a paradise for shopaholics who can bag some great deals. Jeans, sportswear and sports equipment are all relatively cheap, as are American cosmetic brands, leather goods, glasses, electronics and household goods. Furthermore, Oregon doesn't have **sales tax** on consumer goods, so shopping in Portland is a real bargain!

Sizes
Sizes are bigger in the US, so if you usually buy Medium (M) T-shirts, then in the US you will probably need to buy a Small (S).
Take care when buying bed linens, because bed and pillow sizes can vary between countries. Bed linen measurements in the US are in inches. ♿*Units of measure p. 118.*

SMOKING

Legislation concerning tobacco is extremely strict. **Smoking is forbidden** in public areas and on public transportation, as well as in most restaurants, bars, clubs, etc. Cigarettes are quite expensive in the US, although prices vary from one state to next and between stores.

TAXIS

Portland taxis are **yellow**. The pick-up charge is $3, and it's $2.90 per mile.

Broadway Cab – ✆ (503) 333 3333 – www.broadwaycab.com.
Radio Cab Company – ✆ (503) 227 1212 – www.radiocab.net.
Green Cab & Green Shuttle – ✆ 877 853 3577 or ✆ (503) 234 1414 – www.greentrans.com.
Union Cab – ✆ (503) 222 2222 – www.unioncabpdx.com.

Ridesharing companies
Lyft – lyft.com
Wingz – wingz.com
Uber – uber.com

TEMPERATURE

Temperatures are given in degrees **Fahrenheit**; 0°C is 32°F. To loosely convert Fahrenheit to Celsius, subtract 30 and then divide by 2. For example, if it's 70°F, subtract 30 to get 40, then divide by 2 to get 20°C, which is 68°F.

TIPPING

Tips are part of employees' salaries, as the minimum wage is low, so tipping is a must.
In **hotels**, leave $3-$5 **per night** for the housekeeper, with a word of thanks making it clear that the tip is for him/her. A porter or bellhop should be given $1 to $2 per suitcase. Between $1 and $2 should also be left for valets.
In **restaurants**, you should leave between 15 and 20% of the total bill *before* tax. At **bars**, tip $1 per drink. At restaurants, sometimes a tip is already included in the bill, under the total, in a section titled gratuity (you'll see a percentage). Make sure you check the bill first to see if tip has been included. If you pay by card, the receipt will have

a line for the tip. Write the amount of tip you want to leave and add it to the total bill before signing. For example, if your bill is $30 before tax, $5 is a reasonable tip. Whatever you leave, fill in the total box by hand to avoid any misunderstandings once you leave. You can also pay by card and the tip in cash; if you do so, write CASH on the tip line.

TOURIST OFFICES

Tourist offices
Portland Visitor Center – *C5* – 877 SW Taylor St. – ✆ (503) 275 8355 – www.travelportland.com – Mon-Fri. 8:30am-5:30pm, Sat 10am-4pm, Sun (from May to Oct) 10am-2pm. In Director Park (Downtown), it has loads of brochures and information packets.
TravelPortland.com: useful, intuitive and includes a calendar of events.

Information in Downtown
Sidewalk Ambassadors – Tue-Sat 10am-6pm. A team from the city government, on bikes and dressed in green, hands out free city maps and information to tourists.

UNITS OF MEASURE

In the US, the imperial system is used for measurements rather than metric:
1 pound (lb) = 0.45 kg
1 ounce (oz) = 28.35 g
1 pint (pt) = 0.47 l
1 gallon (gal) = 3.79 liters
1 inch (in) = 2.54 cm
1 foot (ft) = 30 cm
1 yard (yd) = 0.91 m
1 mile (mi) = 1.6 km

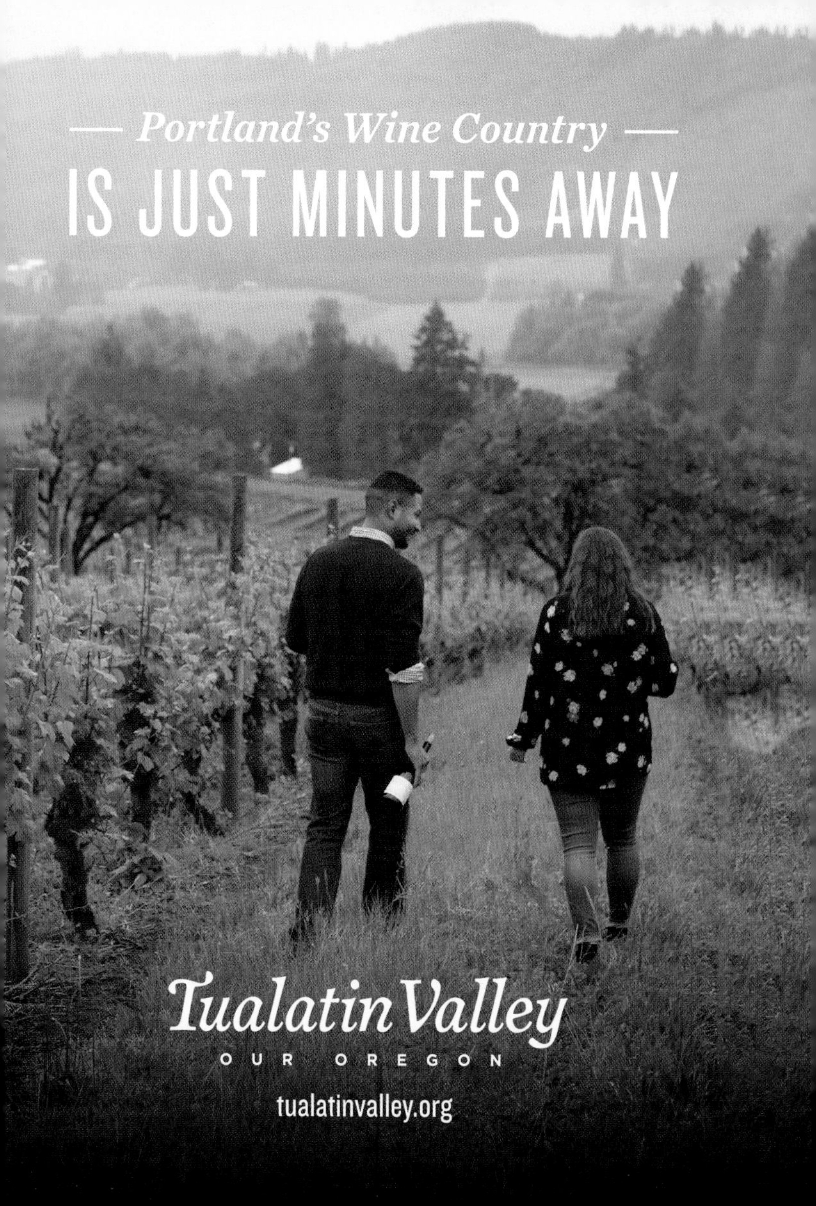
— Portland's Wine Country —
IS JUST MINUTES AWAY
Tualatin Valley
OUR OREGON
tualatinvalley.org

Festivals and cultural events

KEY DATES

January
▶ **Chinese New Year at Lan Su Chinese Gardens** – www.lansugarden.org. In late January to early February (based on the lunar calendar). For two weeks, you'll find New Year celebrations in full swing at the Lan Su Gardens in Chinatown.

February
▶ **Portland International Film Festival** – www.nwfilm.org. The biggest international film festival in Oregon takes place during the last two weeks of February .

▶ **Portland Winter Light Festival** – www.pdxwlf.com. At the start of the month, this festival brightens up the winter gloom.

▶ **The One Moto Show** – www.the1moto.com. At the start of the

month, motorcycle races take place alongside biker events and concerts.

▶ **PDX Jazz Festival** – www.pdxjazz.com. This festival takes place at the end of the month, with concerts from renowned musicians and free jam sessions.

March
▶ **Portland Dining Month** – www.portlanddiningmonth.com. All month, more than 100 of the city's best restaurants serve three-course menus for $33.

April
▶ **Design Week Portland** – www.designportland.org. In mid-April, a full week is dedicated to design, architecture, fashion, landscaping, cinema and handicrafts. There are conferences, guided tours, film screenings, master classes and open studios.

▶ **Soul'd Out Music Festival** – www.souldoutfestival.com. In mid-April, you'll find this soul music festival in venues across Portland.

May
▶ **Portland Rose Festival** – www.rosefestival.org. From late May to early June, the City of Roses pays tribute to its name with a festival exploding with color: parades of rose-covered floats, boat races, fireworks and, of course, the selection of a Rose Queen.

Entertainment on wheels!
*Portland's roller derby league, the **Rose City Rollers** (www.rosecityrollers.com), puts on a great show. They won the international championship in 2018. Don't miss your chance to grab seats at one of these extremely physical women's races - where opposing teams crash into each other - at their stomping ground, the Hangar, in Oaks Amusement Park, south of the city.*

▶ **Cinco de Mayo** – www.cincodemayo.org. The biggest Mexican festival in Portland, based on the traditional Mexican Cinco de Mayo celebrations, is centered on May 5. Enjoy three days of food, concerts of Mexican music, dancing and handicrafts.

June

▶ **Portland Pride** – www.pridenw.org. Pride is a worldwide annual LGBTQ event in mid-June. Enjoy a lively and colorful parade and concerts.

▶ **World Naked Bike Ride** – www.worldnakedbikeride.org. At the end of June, 10,000 cyclists take to their bikes at night while baring it all.

July

▶ **Oregon Brewers Festival** – www.oregonbrewfest.com. At the end of the month, go to the Tom McCall Waterfront Park and discover the meticulous work of local brewers at this beer festival.

▶ **Waterfront Blues Festival** – www.waterfrontbluesfest.com. At the beginning of the month, this renowned blues festival also coincides with the breathtaking July 4th (American Independence Day) fireworks.

August

▶ **Pickathon Festival** – pickathon.com. Pendarvis Farm in Happy Valley (16 miles from Portland). At the start of the month, this eco-friendly rock and folk fest, well loved by families, is held in the forest, with stages made from branches!

▶ **Adult Soapbox Derby** – www.soapboxracer.com. For a day in mid-August, teams zoom down the slopes of Mount Tabor in these "soapbox" cars, made out of anything and everything.

September

▶ **Time-Based Art (TBA) Festival** – www.pica.org/tba. At the start of the month, for ten days, contemporary artists (musicians, artists, dancers) put on performances and interactive installations around the city.

▶ **Feast Portland** – www.feastportland.com. In mid-September, there are three days of culinary events in different areas around the city.

October

▶ **Portland Night Market** – www.pdxnm.com. For two nights, this large food market takes over Central Eastside (100 SE Alder St.), bringing together the best chefs and food carts in town, as well as crafts and decor stands. This event also reappears in February, April, July and December.

November

▶ **Portland Book Festival** – www.literary-arts.org. This festival, which takes place at the beginning of November, features book signings, lectures and concerts.

▶ **Wine Country Thanksgiving** – www.willamettewines.com. At the end of the month, for Thanksgiving, over 130 Willamette Valley wineries open their doors for visits and tastings.

December

▶ **Holiday Ale Festival** – www.holidayale.com. In late November/early December, this beer festival takes place under the soaring Christmas tree in Pioneer Courthouse Square.

Find out more

Portland in the twilight, Mount Hood in the background
© Travel Portland

History of Portland

FROM CHINOOKS TO OREGON TRAIL SETTLERS

Portland's Willamette Valley was once flooded by the melting **Missoula Glacial Lake**. Two native tribes of Chinook fisher-gatherers, the Multnomah and the Clackamas, lived here until settlers following the Lewis and Clark expedition violently drove them off their land.

In 1803, President **Thomas Jefferson** sent Meriwether Lewis to explore the waterways up the Missouri River to encourage trade across the continent. In the 1830s, thousands of colonists of European descent set out on the route opened by Lewis and his partner William Clark, the famous **Oregon Trail**.

HEADS OR TAILS: THE FOUNDING OF PORTLAND

In the beginning, Portland was little more than a trading post located about 10 miles from the mouth of the Willamette River. Aware of the economic potential of this location, the colonists **William Overton** and **Asa Lovejoy** decided to buy the land. In 1845, Overton sold his share to **Francis W. Pettygrove**, who renamed the fledgling town after his birthplace in Maine: Portland. Legend has it that the two men, who both wanted to name the site after their respective hometowns (Lovejoy was from Boston), decided by flipping a coin: the famous Portland Penny. Today,

the Penny is on display at the Oregon Historical Society (*p. 18*).

A PORT TOWN WITH A NOTORIOUS REPUTATION

In 1851, the town only had 800 inhabitants. But from the mid-19th century onward, Portland grew at an extraordinary rate because of its river access to the Pacific Ocean via the **Columbia** and **Willamette** and its fertile agricultural land in the Tualatin, Columbia and Willamette valleys. The town's boom accelerated in the 1880s with the arrival of the railway. Portland's location, at the confluence of two rivers, made it an ideal shipping port.

However, as trade flourished with China and other then-distant lands, Portland gained a notorious reputation. Prostitution, alcoholism and crime reigned in the Old Town/Chinatown underworld (*p. 25*). Still, immigrants continued to arrive from all over the world, looking to make their fortunes through shipping, agriculture, timber or gold. Portland remained the largest **port town** in the Pacific Northwest until the 1890s, when it was stripped of this title by Seattle. At the time, Portland had 46,385 inhabitants.

FROM THRIVING INDUSTRY TO START-UPS

In the first half of the 20th century, Portland continued to grow at a

Portland, the city of many names

*City of Roses, Stumptown, Bridge Town, Beervana, PDX, Little Beirut, P-Town, RIP City...these are just a few of the ways in which Portlanders affectionately refer to their city. The name **City of Roses** has two possible origins. In the 1870s, Leo Samuel, the Portlander who founded Oregon Life Insurance, always left a pair of shears outside his garden so that passers-by could cut off a rose to brighten their buttonholes. The other story is the mayor's decision to put on a rose festival in 1907, a festival that still takes place today (☝ p. 121). As for the nickname **Stumptown**, this originated in the 1840s. To accommodate the expanding city, trees were felled to make way for new roads. However, the workers left the stumps behind and they dotted the roads for several decades. Portland has also been baptized **Bridge Town** because of the twelve bridges that span the Willamette in the city center.*

© Travel Portland

Bridges over the Willamette

125

spectacular rate, and by 1930, it had 300,000 inhabitants. During the Second World War, estimates indicate that 150,000 people arrived to work in the **shipyards**. In the 1940s and 1950s, organized crime continued to plague Portland.

In the 1960s, following the surge of counter-culture in San Francisco, Portland experienced a similar boom with its hippie scene. With the Crystal Ballroom (☝ p. 92) as its epicenter, the hippie movement gave birth to a libertarian, community spirit that would last through the decades. Today, it can be seen in the food

co-ops, independent radio stations, and Portland's defense of Native American and LGBTQ rights. The 1970s saw environmental concerns taking root, due in part to Oregon governor Tom McCall's environmentally friendly urban planning project (☝ p. 128). Although the 1980s recession hit the city hard, since Intel's arrival in 1995, Portland has become popular with other start-ups, while retaining its appeal among young people searching for alternative lifestyles. With its citizens' average age a mere 36, Portland takes full advantage of its inhabitants' dynamism!

A green way of life

Once an industrial city infamous for its pollution, Portland under Governor **Tom McCall** (1913–1983) became a standard-bearer for the US environmental movement. Portland has been a leader in urban planning since 1972, when its model for the city center set out a series of guidelines for development, architecture and public transportation. The environment is always at the heart of inhabitants' and local authorities' concerns, both on a small and large scale.

GREEN MOBILITY

126

The Harbor Drive freeway, which ran along the western riverbank and divided Portland through its center, was demolished in the 1970s, replaced by the leafy **Tom McCall Waterfront Park** (♿ *p. 38*). It's perfect for taking a stroll or going for a bike ride. With 350 miles of bike lanes, Portlanders are truly avid cyclists: more than 6% of the population use bikes for their daily commute. Portland is also one of the few US towns with a high-quality, well-developed network of public transportation, allowing residents to go car-free. Also, the first US car-sharing firm, Zipcar, was born right here in Portland.

GREEN ARCHITECTURE

In the 1970s, in efforts to become the greenest city in the country, and modeled on the example set by Scandinavian countries, Portland launched a number of huge **eco-district** construction projects. The buildings on these sites were water and energy self-sufficient, built out of local materials and in accordance with environmental standards. In another proactive and ambitious project, the city decided to make it mandatory for new office and accommodation buildings to have green roofs.

Garbage management

*In 1971, the **Bottle Bill**, the first of its kind in the US, obliged retailers to refund a deposit for all empty bottles brought back to the store. Today, Portland has an impressive tally for a city of its size, recycling over 70% of its waste!*

Unique architecture

TURN OF THE 19TH CENTURY

With a surge in economic development, commercial buildings grew increasingly ornate from the 1850s onwards. Architects adorned their buildings with more and more sculpted decorations and, by the late 19th century, the city had one of the highest concentrations of **cast-iron buildings** in the US, alongside New York. With columns, pilasters, depictions of humans and animals, as well as a whole range of stone-imitation moldings, these buildings looked more European than those of many towns in the western US. The city's population grew between 1880 and 1930, which led to the construction of a number of the **wooden houses** so characteristic of the Pacific Northwest. The styles of the time were inspired by English (Queen Anne) or colonial architecture and are fairly eclectic, with large houses like the **Pittock Mansion**, Foulkes, 1914 (👆 *p. 34*) and the **Lloyd Frank Estate**, Brookman, 1924 (👆 *p. 46*). The Prairie style, associated with Frank Lloyd Wright and Louis Sullivan in Chicago, can hardly be found in Oregon, with one notable exception by John Virginius Bennes (1914), **Maegley House**, located in a neighborhood with many old houses.

Furthermore, in 1963, Frank Lloyd Wright designed **Gordon House**, an exceptional house to the south of Portland (*thegordonhouse.org*).

TWO KEY MODERNIST ARCHITECTS FROM OREGON

In 1936, **John Yeon** (1910–1994) found inspiration in Oregon's splendid natural surroundings to design **Watzek House**, one of the most beautiful houses in the western US (*yeoncenter.uoregon. edu*). **Pietro Belluschi** (1899–1994) has designed buildings all over the world, including the MetLife Building in New York. In Portland, he designed the first extensive expansion of the Portland Art Museum (👆 *p. 21*), and in 1938 he designed another iconic house, **Sutor House**, which has recently been restored (*not open to the public*).

SMALL SCALE

There aren't many soaring skyscrapers in Portland. The highest is the white **Wells Fargo** building (546 feet) in Downtown (*1300 SW 5th Ave.*), dating from 1972.

The city continues to develop **environmentally friendly** housing with a creative side, as seen in the murals on the **Fair-Haired Dumbbell** apartments on East Burnside Street (2017), across from the Burnside bridge.

Rebel arts

The slogan "Keep Portland Weird" can be found proudly displayed on walls throughout the city. The "weirdness" referred to is the city's rejection of mainstream, mass culture; Portland has become a real cradle of US counter-culture.

INDIE ROCK

Unlike Seattle, which rose to fame with the grunge movement, Portland's attraction has been its low rents and a local scene encouraging healthy competition, rather than any movement in particular. Many musicians have made Portland their home (**☚** *p. 13*), which has led to the opening of more and more clubs and concert halls (**☚** *Music scenes, p. 92*), and the establishment of **independent labels**. Basements became makeshift recording studios, and there were suddenly more events and creative exchange. Portlander artists, whether native, exiles or adopted, include: The Shins, Gossip and its singer Beth Ditto, Elliott Smith, The Decemberists, Pink Martini, The Dandy Warhols, She & Him (the actor Zooey Deschanel's band), M. Ward, Chromatics, and many more.

INDEPENDENT CINEMA

From the late 80s, **Gus Van Sant** became the leading figure of the independent movie scene with films like *Drugstore Cowboy* (1980), *My Own Private Idaho* (1991) and *Don't Worry, He Won't Get Far on Foot* (2017) featuring marginalized figures or rebel actors from Portland's underground scene. The leader of New Queer Cinema, **Todd Haynes**, who lives in Portland, changed the face of independent US cinema by giving LGBTQ-identifying actors starring roles in his films, such as *Poison* (1991) and *Carol* (2015). Unusually for a country of multiplex cinemas that only show blockbusters or family comedies, here, there are many **independent cinemas**, offering daring art-house and experimental films and serving beer and pizza: Laurelhurst Theater (2735 E. Burnside), Bagdad Theater (3702 SE Hawthorne Blvd), Cinema 21 (616 NW 21st Ave.) and even one with a daycare for the audience's little ones (Academy Theater – 7818 SE Stark St.).

Portland had its own TV show from 2011-2018, **Portlandia**, which painted an affectionately mocking portrait of the hipster community. Matt Groening, the father of *The Simpsons*, is also from Portland.

MURALS

In Portland, **street art** is encouraged and, to some extent, organized by the city. Incredible colorful murals cover the walls of former warehouses, abandoned industrial buildings or the doors of corrugated-iron warehouses. Street artists, selected and funded by civic leaders, unleash their creativity to brighten up the streets.

In 1982, murals began popping up throughout the streets of Portland

© Jim Fullan/Travel Portland

Bagdad Theater

thanks to the collective of anonymous artists **Gorilla Wallflare**. Their wall painted with a giant banana and the slogan "Art Fills the Void" is the oldest mural in Portland, on the corner of Southeast 12th Ave. and Southeast Division St. The second-oldest mural in the city is the Black Pride Malcolm X Mural, in Alberta Arts District (on the corner of Northeast 17th Ave. and Northeast Alberta St.). Created by **Lewis Harris** in 1984 and restored in 2015, it features Malcolm X, leader of the Black Panthers. The largest mural in the US covers the 43,485 sq feet of the Portland Memorial Mausoleum, found in the eccentric, tree-lined streets of Sellwood. 🕐 Murals by Faith47 *(p. 21)* and Fin Dac *(p. 43)*.

Rock out every night of the week

Portland is a hotbed of indie music (🕐 The musicians who call Portland home, p.13). Bands and singers perform at venues across the city seven nights a week. Here's where to catch them. For more intel, see 🕐 Nightlife, p. 92)

- *Aladdin Theater*
- *Al's Den*
- *Doug Fir*
- *Crystal Ballroom*
- *Roseland Ballroom*
- *Wonder Ballroom*

Foodie paradise

Restaurants with tattooed chefs, trendy junk food, food carts on every corner, natural wine bars, microbreweries...in Portland, good food is taken extremely seriously. Here, vegetarians, vegans and locavores will find plenty of options. The city doesn't follow any rules when it comes to food: you can find something to eat at any hour, night or day, and dine in a restaurant wearing sweatpants. Inspired by the bountiful local larder, many young chefs have set up restaurants here, making Portland one of the leading hubs of modern US cuisine.

MOBILE KITCHENS

Since the 2000s, **food carts** have multiplied through the streets of Portland, and today the city has more than 500 of them. Clustered into pods, often in outdoor parking lots, they usually stay in the same spot. You can find street food from around the world: Argentina, South Korea, Scotland, Georgia and South Africa. A popular lunch option for locals, they are found in Downtown, near the offices and shopping malls, and in urban neighborhoods (*www. foodcartsportland.com*). While they are a symbol of Portland, the food carts are still prey to gentrification. What was the largest pod in the world, Alder Street, is now gone.

LOCAVORE CHEFS

Mushrooms from the wooded hillsides of Mount Hood, fish and shellfish from the Pacific Coast, the celebrated dairy herds of Tillamook and fresh vegetables and meat from 35,000 Oregon farms keep Portland chefs and their customers (increasingly concerned about reducing their carbon footprints) happy. The high priest of US cuisine and a Portlander by birth, **James Beard** (1903–1985) was already a dedicated locavore when,

From farm to fork

*Portland, a culinary and locavore city, hosts many **farmers markets** from early spring to late fall. The main ones are found in the Cultural District (👣 p. 86). Go exploring and you'll discover stands with white truffles, charcuterie, cheese, homemade pastries, fresh fruit juice, fruit and vegetables, and hazelnuts, an Oregon specialty. The reason that the fruit and vegetable stands are particularly swamped is because a high proportion of Portlanders are vegetarian (in Portland you'll often find it in property ads: "Looking for a friendly and vegetarian tenant!"). Here, you can make the most of the family ambiance, sitting on the grass, listening to live music and sampling delicious dishes.*
👣 *www.portlandfarmersmarket.org*

in the 1950s, he extolled the benefits of cooking using local products, particularly Oregon's fish and shellfish. Following in Beard's footsteps, Portland chefs like **Naomi Pomeroy** (Beast), **Cathy Whims** (Nostrana) and **Vitaly Paley** (Paley's Place) make environmentally friendly, delicious fare.

THE ART OF JUNK FOOD

In Portland, bars serving hard liquor have to offer a menu of at least three hot and cold snacks. Many local establishments have used this opportunity to become gastropubs, bringing together high quality restaurant food and the atmosphere of a bar. But Portland wouldn't be Portland without its junk food devoured in the early hours after a boozy night out. Try some tater tots (deep-fried potato croquettes) or pizza, which, as a veritable institution of the city, you can find just about anywhere. In Portland you can find delicious junk food made from fresh, local, and often organic products.

CRAFT DRINKING

Today, Portland has a total of 75 **microbreweries**—even more than Cologne, the world's long-undisputed beer capital! Portlanders will never be happy with a supermarket beer when they can choose from a long menu of IPAs, dark, blond and amber beers at their local bars for just a couple of extra cents.

More expensive, but also increasingly popular are **Oregon wines** (♿ *p. 54*), organic and natural. With over 170,000

© Jamie Francis/Travel Portland

Base Camp Brewing Company

133

acres of vineyards, pinot noir is Oregon's signature variety, followed by pinot gris with nearly 3,400 acres. In Portland, coffee is an art form and is tasted in the same way as wines. **Third wave cafés** are independent establishments with carefully selected beans. These cafés have replaced second wave establishments, with their standardized brands and mass-consumption profits. At Portland's coffee shops, the barista is queen and the morning takes on a solemn character when denizens squeeze into cafés for their prized coffee and homemade pastries.

Index

134

W

Y

Maps

Inside

Detachable map

Photo credits

Page 4

Portland Japanese Garden: © Jonathan Ley/Travel Portland
Portland Art Museum: © Portland Art Museum
Portland Saturday Market: © Jamie Francis/Travel Portland
Pearl District: © cosmonaut/iStockphoto.com
International Rose Test Garden: © Jakub Zajic/Shutterstock

Page 5

Oregon Museum of Science and Industry: © Checubus/Shutterstock
Lan Su Chinese Garden: © artran/iStockphoto.com
Mount Hood: © Bryan Nightingale/iStockphoto.com
Powell's City of Books: © Christopher Onstott/Travel Portland
Ecola State Park and Cannon Beach: © Don White/iStockphoto.com

Symbols in the guide

★★★ Worth a special journey   ★★ Worth a detour   ★ Interesting

Hotels and Restaurants

9 rms	Number of rooms
bc	Beverage menu included
▭▭	Payment by credit card
⊅	Credit cards not accepted
▤	Air conditioning in room
✕	Restaurant in hotel
♟	Alcohol served
⌇	Swimming pool

Symbols

ﻝ	Also see
♿	Disabled Access
😐	A bit of advice / consider
😀	Recommended
A2 B	Map coordinates

Maps and Plans

MONUMENTS AND SITES

▲†	Catholic Church
▲†	Protestant church - other temple
▨	Synagogue
▽ ☐	Mosque
ⵏ ◎	Calvary, wayside cross - Fountain
●━●━■	Rampart - Tower - Gate
ѱ	Viewpoint
▼	Observation area
∩	Quarry

INFORMATION

🛈	Tourist information
P P	Parking - Park-and-Ride
⏝ Ⓜ	Tramway - Underground - Métro
🚆 🚌	Train station - Coach (bus) station
▪━▪━▪━▪	Cable cars
▫┅┿┅▫	Funicular - rack railway
🚂	Tourist train
◎ ▨	Post office - Covered market
⚓	Ferry service: cars and passengers
⛴	Passengers only

ADDITIONAL SYMBOLS

══ ══	Motorway - Other primary route
▭▭ ▭▭	Pedestrian street
⁑⁑⁑⁑	Unsuitable for traffic - restrictions
▫▫▫▫ ‖‖‖	Escalator
-----	Footpath
Ⓑ Ⓕ	Car - Ferry
△	Drawbridge

SPORTS AND RECREATION

⛱ ⛱	Swimming: open air - covered
◯ 〇	Stadium
🐎	Racecourse
⚓	Marina - Sailing center

ABBREVIATIONS

H	Town Hall		P	Local authority offices
J	Law courts		POL.	Police station
M	Museum		T	Theatre

139

THE GREEN GUIDE short-stays **Portland**

Editorial Director	Cynthia Ochterbeck
Editor	Sophie Friedman
Translator	Becky Stoakes
Production Manager	Natasha George
Cartography	Peter Wrenn, Theodor Cepraga
Picture Editor	Yoshimi Kanazawa
Interior Design	Laurent Muller
Layout	Natasha George

Contact Us

Michelin Travel and Lifestyle North America
One Parkway South
Greenville, SC 29615
USA
travel.lifestyle@us.michelin.com

Michelin Travel Partner
Hannay House
39 Clarendon Road
Watford, Herts WD17 1JA
UK
✆01923 205240
travelpubsales@uk.michelin.com
www.viamichelin.co.uk

Special Sales

For information regarding bulk sales,
customized editions and premium sales,
please contact us at:
travel.lifestyle@us.michelin.com

YOUR OPINION IS ESSENTIAL
TO IMPROVING OUR PRODUCTS

Help us by answering the
questionnaire on our website:
satisfaction.michelin.com

PORTLAND
REGION

TRAVEL  OREGON

 MICHELIN

Michelin Travel Partner

Société par actions simplifiées au capital de 15 044 940 EUR
27 cours de l'Île Seguin - 92100 Boulogne Billancourt (France)
R.C.S. Nanterre 433 677 721

© Michelin Travel Partner
ISBN 978-2-067245-75-4
Printed: December 2019
Printer: ESTIMPRIM